Flora

I was but a Child

PREVIOUSLY PUBLISHED IN THIS SERIES BY YAD VASHEM:

Enzo Tayar, *Days of Rain*

Alan Elsner, *Guarded by Angels: How My Father and Uncle Survived Hitler and Cheated Stalin*

Isabelle Choko, Frances Irwin, Lotti Kahana-Aufleger, Margit Raab Kalina, Jane Lipski, *Stolen Youth: Five Women's Survival in the Holocaust*

Hadassah Rosensaft, *Yesterday My Story*

Gabriel Mermall, Norbert J. Yasharoff, *By the Grace of Strangers: Two Boys' Rescue During the Holocaust*

E.H. (Dan) Kampelmacher, *Fighting for Survival*

Hersch Altman, *On the Fields of Loneliness*

PUBLISHED BY THE UNITED STATES HOLOCAUST MEMORIAL MUSEUM:

Adam Boren, *Journey Through the Inferno*

Margaret Bergmann Lambert, *By Leaps and Bounds*

Joseph E. Tenenbaum, *Legacy and Redemption; A Life Renewed*

Flora
I was but a Child

FLORA M. SINGER

YAD VASHEM AND
THE HOLOCAUST SURVIVORS' MEMOIRS PROJECT
New York • Jerusalem

This book is published by Yad Vashem, the Holocaust Martyrs' and Heroes' Remembrance Authority, c/o American Society for Yad Vashem, 500 Fifth Avenue, 42nd floor, New York, New York 10110-4299, and P.O.B. 3477, Jerusalem 91034, Israel

www.yadvashem.org

and

The Holocaust Survivors' Memoirs Project
in association with the World Federation of Bergen-Belsen Associations, Inc.

The Holocaust Survivors' Memoirs Project, an initiative of Nobel Peace Prize laureate Elie Wiesel, was launched through a generous grant from Random House, Inc., New York, New York.

Cover photos and all other photographs courtesy of Flora M. Singer

Library of Congress Cataloging-in-Publication Data

Singer, Flora M. 1930-
Flora : I was but a child / Flora M. Singer ; preface by Theodore E. McCarrick ; foreword by Sir Martin Gilbert.
    p. cm.
  "In association with the World Federation of Bergen-Belsen Associations, Inc."
  ISBN 0-9760739-8-6 (alk. paper)
  1. Singer, Flora M. 1930- 2. Jews--Belgium--Antwerp--Biography--Juvenile literature. 3. Hidden children (Holocaust)--Belgium--Biography--Juvenile literature. 4. Holocaust, Jewish (1939-1945)--Belgium--Personal narratives--Juvenile literature. 5. Holocaust survivors--New York (State)--New York--Biography--Juvenile literature. 6. Righteous Gentiles in the Holocaust--Belgium--Biography--Juvenile literature. 7. Antwerp (Belgium)--Biography--Juvenile literature. I. Title.
DS135.B43S567 2007
940.53'18092--dc22
[B]

2007007072

Typesetting: Judith Sternberg
Produced by Artplus

Printed in Jerusalem, Israel.

Michael Berenbaum,
Former Director of the
Research Institute of the
U.S. Holocaust Memorial
Museum and Author

"*Flora, I Was But a Child* is a moving memoir of a young Jewish girl living, hiding and surviving in German-occupied Belgium during World War II. Flora's story is gripping, told without self-pity, but with deep gratitude toward the many people who helped her mother, herself and her two younger sisters to survive, and with appreciation for the anguish of the time and the cost of survival.

Flora, I Was But a Child is a work not only to be read, but, as its author, to be cherished."

Abraham H. Foxman,
National Director,
Anti-Defamation League,
and Author

"Flora Singer's story is important because it tells us what must never be forgotten that when good people stand up against evil, lives are saved. Flora's moving account of her family in those terrible times and how she lived as a 'hidden child,' survived the war and became a teacher and witness, is a significant contribution to the understanding not only of history, but of how individuals can make a difference."

Fred S. Zeidman,
Chairman, United States
Holocaust Memorial
Council

"When I first heard Flora Singer tell her compelling story of escaping, hiding and being rescued from the Nazis, I felt privileged to meet this woman of exceptional courage and optimism. Now readers will finally have an opportunity to learn of her bravery as a young girl in Belgium and her eventual immigration to the United States. We have much to learn from Flora's experiences, her humanity and her spirit."

ACKNOWLEDGEMENTS

This story is a tribute to my dear mother, Fani Mendelovits, whose love and tenacity saved me and my two sisters, Charlotte and Betty, from arrest and probable death at the hands of the Nazi occupiers in Belgium. This book is dedicated to her and to the many people – Belgian, French and German – who went out of their way, risking their lives to help us live through the Holocaust.

This story is also dedicated to my family members who did not survive.

I will never forget them.

I thank my husband, Jack, and my daughter, Sandy Landsman, for their love, help and support in writing this story. I would not have been able to complete it without their active encouragement and that of the rest of my family and my many friends. I particularly want to recognize the efforts of Mel Hecker, Don and Marcia McComb, Peter Black, Benton Arnowitz, Judy Cohen, Jerry Rehm, Ben Nachman, Serge Wauthier, David Silberklang, and Daniella Zaidman-Mauer.

With many thanks,

Flora

CONTENTS

PREFACE

By Cardinal Theodore E. McCarrick

Flora Mendelovits Singer's story is one of the survival of a courageous and remarkably blessed young woman who endured the terrible ordeal of the Holocaust, and yet found so much human kindness in the midst of overwhelming fear and hatred, it enabled her to rejoice in the goodness of special people. Her inner strength and her trust in good people come through these pages as a song of hope amidst a background of evil.

In her later years in America, Flora was an active volunteer at the United States Holocaust Memorial Museum, where she became a compelling speaker who ably shared her extraordinary experiences with people across the United States. It is important that she has now written down those memories so that they shall live after her. In addition to being an inspiration, hers is a great adventure story and a story of great love – the love she had for her parents and her sisters.

It is a compelling lesson to learn of the tragedy and suffering of a courageous people, and of a few men and women of deep faith who, at great risk to themselves, offered help, and oftentimes safety and survival, to as many of their Jewish neighbors as they could. As a priest, I rejoice in the example of Fr. Bruno Reynders, a Benedictine Monk, who rallied others and found a way to help so many – especially children – escape death and torture.

Flora was one of those child survivors. The beautiful love of some Christian nuns speaks of devotion and hope and the wonderful understanding that we are all brothers and sisters in God's one human family. They understood that we always need to care for each other, whatever our religion, our race, or our nationality, and so Flora was saved. Her story is surely worth reading.

Cardinal Theodore E. McCarrick
Archbishop of Washington, D.C. (retired)

FOREWORD

By Sir Martin Gilbert

N o Holocaust story is the same as any other. Each person's experience adds something to our knowledge of that terrible time, and Flora Singer has written a memoir of the utmost charm and sensitivity. This memoir is no exception to the rule, and starts with a childhood journey in 1937 from Antwerp to Romania to visit her mother's family – including her grandfather, Moishe. Crossing borders, including the German border, and passing through Berlin, held no hazards in the pre-war years for those with their documents in order, but the young Flora did see for the first time the Swastika armband, and people being escorted off the train "by men wearing uniforms."

Every vignette of pre-war Jewish life is precious, as is the recollection here of outings in the countryside within sight of the Carpathian Mountains. This was the first time that Flora met her *Zeyde* (grandfather) and it was to be the last. "He perished in Auschwitz, as did most of the other members of our beautiful family."

On the eve of war, Flora's father was able to leave Belgium for Canada. The war made it impossible for the rest of the family to follow. Flora survived in hiding in Belgium; those experiences in hiding form the central part of her memoir. Throughout, her mother's love and concern shine through. Her mother would even cross into northern France to find food and smuggle it back. Flora, too, made that journey across the border and back.

The young Flora, who was ten years old in 1940, saw terrible scenes. On one occasion in Antwerp, watching from a second-floor window, she saw young Nazi sympathizers kick an old Jewish shopkeeper to death. Their last act in this cruel torment was to jump on the man's stomach and do a dance on his body.

Among the righteous gentiles in this account is Karl Frischbier, a German soldier who knew the family before the war. At a crucial moment, he warned them to leave Antwerp. Their next hiding place was Brussels, where they masqueraded as non-Jews. Flora describes the perils they faced with bated breath, drawing the reader into the fear and uncertainty. Forced to leave Brussels, Flora and her two sisters found refuge in a convent in a small village, where there were many moments of anxiety and danger. During some of the sermons at Sunday Mass, Flora recalled that the priest made statements expressing his sorrow for the tribulations suffered by the Jewish people at the hands of the Nazis. But he would then say, with a sad expression on his face, that unfortunately today's Jews were paying for the sins of their fathers.

Returning to Brussels, Flora and her sisters rejoined their mother. The three sisters were then taken to another convent under the watchful eye of one of the great saviors of the Jewish people, Père (Father) Bruno. Flora Singer's account of life in the convent with her two sisters is absorbing and uplifting. Their life in hiding depended entirely on the devoted and continual care and vigilance of others, and the nuns, led by the Reverend Mother Marie Chrysostome, were remarkable. When the Gestapo seized Flora Singer's uncle, aunt and cousin, they took in her mother; thus mother and daughters survived.

Yet even in the convent there were moments of danger. Once, one of the residents told Flora's mother: "Jews are dirty, Jews stink, they are thieves, they are sneaky, they have shifty eyes; they are evil..."

In these pages, good triumphs over the real evil: the Nazi determination to destroy all Jewish life in Europe. These pages are a tribute to those who took great risks to thwart the Nazi will. They also show how, in the immediate aftermath of the defeat of Nazism, the survivors struggled against a world that did not automatically want to help them, or know how to do so. The pages describing post-war Europe and the journey to the United States, the reunion with her father, and how she worked in New York's garment district are poignant.

Flora Singer appreciates her good fortune amid all the dangers she encountered. She is able now to visit the graves of both her parents. "I am at peace. No one killed them. They did not vanish without a trace like the millions of victims in the Holocaust. I know where they are buried and they rest in peace."

These pages are a powerful testimony to the Jewish spirit and to the human spirit at a time of darkness and destruction.

INTRODUCTION

Before the War

My name is Flora. When I was seven years old, not long after Passover 1937, Mama decided, and Papa agreed, that she and the children would travel to Romania, the country of Mama and Papa's birth, for a visit with their family. Neither Papa nor Mama had seen any of them since the day they left for Antwerp, Belgium with a group of young people seeking better lives in Western Europe.

By the time that summer arrived, Mama had completed all the travel plans and I was very excited about the adventure – a journey by train to a faraway place where I would finally meet Mama's father, my *Zeyde* (grandpa) Moishe Genut, and my paternal grandmother, Rachel Mendelovits. I also looked forward to meeting the many aunts, uncles and cousins whom I knew only through the vivid stories Mama told us nightly just before bedtime. I was acquainted with the faces of both Mama's and Papa's family members from the photographs Mama had hung on our apartment walls, as well as those neatly placed on the pages of several photo albums she kept in her dresser drawer.

During the First World War, Moishe Genut was drafted to fight on the front, and during his absence, Mama lost her mother, Frimet, to pneumonia. When her Papa returned, he found his eldest daughter, my Aunt Sara, caring for her five younger siblings, including my mother, Fani, and my Aunt Lea. He then married a widow, Pessel-Chava, who had two sons of her own and who now assumed caring for the extended family. My paternal grandfather, Solomon, had also been killed on the front during World War I.

1

David Mendelovits and Fani Davidovits/Genut left Viseu de Sus, Romania (northern Transylvania), to settle in Antwerp, Belgium in late 1927 or early 1928. They were part of a group of about twelve Jewish young friends between the ages of nineteen and twenty-five who had intermittently discussed the prevalent and unceasing antisemitism in their homeland. Concluding that the future looked bleak for Jewish young people in Romania, they looked to establish roots elsewhere, even if that meant leaving behind the families they loved. They were encouraged to leave for Antwerp by friends who preceded them there.

A small western European country of barely twelve million inhabitants, Belgium was ruled by a constitutional monarchy and was unique in many ways. Unlike many other countries, she opened her doors during the difficult years following World War I to welcome immigrants fleeing from oppressive regimes in Eastern Europe. All in all, the people and rulers of this predominantly Catholic country, with the exception of a few radical antisemitic groups, were generally quite tolerant of non-Catholics, and the government supported schools of all faiths and denominations.

The twelve young immigrants were welcomed by the members of the Antwerp Jewish community and were offered temporary lodgings in the homes of several families. They also received help in finding employment and stayed with their host families until they were able to find and maintain their own living quarters.

About a year later, several of the new arrivals paired off and married. The others in the group provided the basic necessities for the weddings: they found wedding outfits for the new couples, and catered the nuptial feasts for their friends.

On May 29, 1929, Fani and David, my parents, married in a religious ceremony under a canopy as dictated by Jewish tradition. Surrounded by all their friends and new acquaintances, they celebrated their union, but sadly without any family members present. In their new home, their friends had become their family. Soon the marriage was blessed by my birth on August 16, 1930. They called me Flora. My sister, Charlotte, was born on March 1, 1933, and Betty was born on June 7, 1936. Papa, a trained carpenter, built up a good business as a custom furniture maker. Although not easy, life in Antwerp was happy and our young family thrived.

Before we left for our special trip to Romania, Mama, in addition to her regular housework, busied herself with shopping for gifts. She had a list and checked off the name of each person after she purchased something for him or her. At my grandfather's request she bought practical items like underwear for the poor children of Viseu de Sus. Her purchases, however, were limited by the amount of luggage she was able to carry. I heard her discuss this problem with Papa as they struggled to pack as many items as they could into the suitcases.

Finally, the day of our departure for Romania arrived. Mama checked all our tickets and documents – and I noticed that her passport included a photograph of all four of us. We closed the suitcases and carried them to the central railroad station, accompanied by Papa. As we walked, I was filled with anticipation, and could not wait to board the train. By the time it pulled into the station, it was dusk. Papa kissed each of us goodbye, then helped us up the steps into the railroad car. We took our seats and looked through the window at the platform below. When the train started to move we waved to Papa and threw him kisses until he was out of sight. Even Betty, only a year old, pressed her little nose against the window to watch Papa disappear. Once the train left the station, we settled back into our compartment.

Betty climbed onto Mama's lap, curled up against her and fell fast asleep. Charlotte fell asleep shortly after that, but I was just too excited to sleep. But as night fell outside the window, the rocking train ride lulled me to sleep, too.

Suddenly, the train stopped. Everyone, with the exception of my two sisters, awakened with a jolt. We had reached the German border on our way to Berlin. There we were to change trains for Prague, Czechoslovakia, where yet another train would take us to Romania. Official-looking men in uniforms boarded the train and went from compartment to compartment to check passengers' passports and other travel documents. When one of the uniformed men came to us, Mama and the other passengers in our compartment opened their bags, pulled out their travel documents, and presented them to the official. He checked the papers, glanced at my sleeping sisters, smiled at me, and then left. The train continued on its way and the rest of the night passed uneventfully.

In Berlin, we changed trains again. Mama checked the board that posted the schedule of departures, destinations, and tracks from which the trains would leave, and then we carried the suitcases to the platform for our connecting train to Prague. We made our way to the correct platform and sat down on one of the benches. Mama opened one of the smaller suitcases filled with food for our journey and took out a few cookies for us to snack on. She told us that we would eat more substantially once we were settled in on the next train. She also told me, as she had many times before, how much she wanted her family members in Romania to meet the three of us.

We spent several hours waiting in the Berlin station. I remember seeing many men in military uniforms and posters displaying swastikas, but I did not know what the swastika was or what it signified. Eventually, we boarded the train for Prague, where we changed trains once more. Each time we changed trains or crossed a border we were subjected to inspection of our travel documents. Fortunately, ours were always in order so we had no problems beyond the inconvenience of train delays while we waited for officials to check all the other passengers' documents. When we saw people being escorted off the train by men in uniform, Mama explained that there were probably problems relating to their documents.

All in all, we took four different trains for two days and two nights before we arrived at our destination.

My maternal grandfather, Moishe, my *Zeyde*, as I learned to call him, was waiting for us at the Viseu de Sus train stop – a wooden platform built alongside the tracks that allowed passengers to descend from the trains. You could see the road beyond, where *Zeyde* sat on his wagon, holding the reins of his team of two horses. As soon as he saw us he climbed down and ran to greet us with arms open wide and a big smile illuminating his bearded face. I looked at the landscape beyond the railroad station and was able to see magnificent mountains. I later learned that they were part of the Carpathian mountain range.

With *Zeyde's* help, Charlotte and I climbed onto the back of the wagon and sat down on wooden benches that were part of the wagon's side railings. Then Mama lifted Betty and handed her to me. I placed her on my lap, holding her securely around the waist in the circle of my arms. After *Zeyde* had lifted and placed our suitcases on the back of the wagon, he and Mama climbed up and sat on the driver's bench immediately behind the horses. *Zeyde* took up the reins, called out an order, and the horses began to pull the wagon along the uneven road. It was a bumpy, exciting ride. I enjoyed it as my eyes, wide with wonder, took in the new and strange scenery. This was the first time in my life that I had ridden in a wagon pulled by real, live horses! It was very different from riding on a "merry-go-round" and much more interesting.

The main road was covered with cobblestones and made for a rough ride. As we drew closer to the actual town of Viseu de Sus, I noticed that some of the smaller roads had no cobblestones – they were simply hard-packed earth. As we passed several farms and orchards, I realized that this was very different from the big modern harbor city I was used to. Even the few people walking along the road looked very different from the people in Antwerp. The local farmers wore heavy-looking work clothes and the women with them wore long, bulky-looking skirts. Most of these women wore their hair tied back in a bun or covered their heads with a kerchief – a babushka, as Mama called it.

As they sat and talked, Mama told *Zeyde* over and over again how much she wanted to come and how much she wanted the whole family to meet her three children. She also wanted our cousins to get to know us. At that time, Charlotte was only four and Betty was just a year old, so the visit to Romania is but a cloudy dream in their memories. As for me, as a seven-year-old, the memory of the trip to my parents' birthplace, where they grew into adulthood, remains sharp in my mind. Mama had often talked about Viseu de Sus, but I could not really visualize it until I was there and could see it with my own eyes. Even now, seventy years later, the images of the town and surrounding countryside are clearly etched in my mind.

We arrived at *Zeyde*'s house where Mama's stepmother, Pessel-Chava, and her stepbrother were waiting to greet us. Afterward, we sat around a long rectangular wooden table in what was a combination dining/sitting room with two windows that looked out onto Mill Street. We noticed a few children trying to look in on us from the street. Pessel-Chava went over to one of the windows and with her hands made a motion to shoo them away.

When I had finished eating and was waiting to be dismissed from the table, I listened to the stories Mama told *Zeyde*. Betty was tired and started to cry, so Mama excused herself to put Betty to bed. It had been a long two days for the little child. Charlotte and I remained at the table with *Zeyde* as he said the grace after the meal. By the time he finished, Mama returned and motioned to Charlotte and me to get up and follow her into the kitchen, where she filled a large bowl with water, carried it into the bedroom, and helped both of us wash up. Then Mama brushed Charlotte's hair while I brushed my own.

She helped us get into our pajamas and put us to bed. The bed we climbed into was a big double bed, quite high from the floor, with a thick mattress and very fluffy down-filled pillows and a duvet. It was cozy and I slept solidly until the next morning, when the sun's shining rays came through the windowpanes and woke me up.

I was the first one up. Mama and Charlotte were still fast asleep next to me and Betty was sitting up in the crib against the wall, about four feet away. I climbed out of bed and went to Betty, who raised her arms to be picked up. I brought her over to the double bed where Mama and Charlotte were waking up. Mama took Betty from me. Before you could blink, Charlotte and I were washed, dressed and ready for our first exciting day, ready to meet many family members and see different and interesting sights.

Zeyde, who tended orchards, took the day off to spend precious time, as he put it, with his daughter and granddaughters. We visited the marketplace to see the vendor's stand where he sold apples, pears and other fruits he and his brothers harvested from their orchards. Some of their produce was wholesaled to other merchants and some of it was dried and then sold. Because *Zeyde* was spending time with us, one of his brothers was minding the stand, and so we got to meet one of our great-uncles. We visited the orchards often during our time in Romania and with *Zeyde*'s help I managed to climb onto the lower tree branches and pick some fruit. The visits to the orchards were quite exciting for this city child, and we had fun visiting other towns and cities where members of Mama's family lived – Czernowitz, Sighet, the capital Bucharest and even Budapest, the capital of Hungary.

Two of Mama's sisters lived in Viseu de Sus with their husbands and families and one lived elsewhere. The relatives on both sides of the family were very Orthodox, so most of Mama's sisters, except Aunt Lea, the youngest sister (who lived in Antwerp, too), wore wigs or other head coverings as prescribed by religious law for married women. Mama and Aunt Lea observed the Shabbat and kept kosher, but balked at cutting their hair after marriage, refusing to don wigs or wear long-sleeved and long dresses during the summer heat.

To please her father while we were in Romania, Mama covered her hair with a headscarf and wore long-sleeved garments – depending on where we went. She did this in order not to shame her father before his neighbors, friends and certain family members. I remember that when I questioned her about this she said we were required to respect the beliefs, feelings and customs of others when we are with them; we must sometimes acquiesce and follow certain rituals, even when we don't totally accept them for ourselves. She said that we must do this with Jewish people, as well as others, as a sign of respect for their religious laws.

My *Zeyde* Moishe was a very intelligent and tolerant man. Although he, himself, was deeply religious and followed all the rules and rituals of our religion, he never criticized or imposed his views on anybody else, not even his own adult children. I remember him saying, and Mama repeated it often, that he raised his children and guided them, and that now that they were adults they made their own decisions as to how they wished to live their lives.

While in Viseu de Sus, I loved going on outings to the cold river that ran just below the Carpathian Mountains. The water was so crystal clear, we could see the bottom and I loved walking and splashing in the river. I also found it fascinating to sit on the banks and watch the women of the town line up along the shore to do the weekly laundry. Each woman sat on her knees, bending over a corrugated scrub board. After rubbing the wet, soapy laundry vigorously against the scrub board, the women rinsed the clothes in the river's clear water before tossing them into baskets at their sides. The women sang and talked to each other, sharing the day's news and gossip until they completed their task. When finished, they placed their scrub boards and supplies on top of their loaded baskets and returned to their homes to hang the clean wash on the clothes lines in their backyards.

As young as I was, I could not help observing that at the riverbank the Christian women sat apart from the Jewish women. Occasionally individuals from each group would speak to each other, but generally the women socialized with their own, and you could tell them apart by their clothing. Though most of the women wore long skirts and babushkas, they wore distinctly different styles. The non-Jewish women's clothing was colorfully embroidered, but the Jewish women wore simple sober dresses in dark colors.

Pessel-Chava was very strict and insisted on total obedience of her rules. She was unfriendly and always wore a scowl on her face, except when her sons would visit and rare warmth would be reflected on her face. But I did not like her and later learned that when Mama was a child, she didn't get along with Pessel-Chava either. *Zeyde*, on the other hand, always had a ready smile for me on his face. He also showed great interest in my stories, and would listen to my adventures at the river, chuckle, and then would ask "And so, tell me, what happened next?" I would miss my *Zeyde* a lot. He was such a wonderful audience, and I loved him dearly.

The time with our family in Romania flew by all too quickly. Before we knew it, it was time to leave. When we climbed aboard the train, Mama was very subdued and quiet. She sat holding a sleeping Betty on her lap while looking out the window. Charlotte and I sat opposite them. When Mama turned toward me, I saw tears slowly sliding down her cheeks. Her gaze met mine and she quickly wiped her tears with the back of her hand. In a low voice, in order not to wake Betty, I asked, "Mama, why are you crying?"

She replied in Yiddish, "Oh, it's nothing, *mamele*. Close your eyes and try to get some sleep." Her answer did not satisfy me, but I was not supposed to question Mama. Charlotte snuggled against my side as I cradled her small body with my arm and she was soon fast asleep.

That summer was the first time my sisters and I met our *Zeyde*. It was also the last. When we were preparing to leave *Zeyde's* cottage, while being hugged and kissed by everyone, Mama had promised to return to see the family with Papa. It was a promise never kept, a visit that would never, could never, take place. *Zeyde* Moishe perished in Auschwitz, as did most of the members of our beautiful and large family.

CHAPTER 1

The Beginning

When we arrived in Antwerp, Papa met us at the Central Railroad Station. He stood on the platform and I was able to see him through the train window as the train slowed to a stop. I was so happy that I forgot my sadness at leaving my *Zeyde* and all my new family members behind. Papa kissed Mama, then Charlotte and me. He took Betty from Mama's arms and picked up one of the suitcases while Mama and I carried the other pieces of luggage. As we made our way out of the railroad station, down the Pelikaanstraat toward the Lange Kievitstraat where we lived, Mama shared some of our experiences with Papa. He was anxious to hear how members of Mama's and his family fared, especially his mother and brothers. Even after we had arrived home and settled back in, Papa and Mama continued talking. They continued talking while Mama unpacked the suitcases and Papa prepared a light supper.

Later, at the table, the conversation continued. I joined in telling Papa about our wonderful *Zeyde* and Mama's mean stepmother. I told him how amazed I was to see all the places Mama had described in the stories she used to tell me just before bedtime. When I saw them, I told Papa, I felt as if I had been there before, that is how vividly Mama had described them. I also told him about the several visits we made to his family, but most of my stories were about Mama's family because we had spent more time with them.

While in Romania, we also visited Mama's sisters, and I told Papa all about our visits to Budapest and Bucharest. One of our best visits in Romania was to Sighet, where, in addition to family members and friends, we also visited Mama's old friend, Lotzi. Lotzi was the young man Mama had wanted to marry before she met Papa, but *Zeyde* was against it because Lotzi was not religious. He did not observe the Sabbath or cover his head as prescribed by Jewish religious law.

For several days Mama and I related our travel adventures and Papa listened, his face reflecting great pleasure at our tales. Even Charlotte, who sat on Papa's lap, shared a few stories with him and brought a wide smile to his face.

During the rest of August, our life resumed its regular routine. Papa left every weekday morning for his furniture shop, and Mama took care of her usual household chores and the paperwork for Papa's business, writing estimates for potential orders, billing clients and so forth. She also began preparing our clothing for school, adjusting hems and checking to make sure all the buttons were secure. I remember enjoying the last few free days of August before school began in September.

Many of my Jewish friends attended a private Jewish school, but Mama and Papa sent me to the public school so that I would be more integrated into Belgian life. I also attended Yiddish school twice during the week in the afternoons and on Sunday mornings, to learn to read and write Yiddish and to learn Jewish history and culture.

On the first day of the public school year 1937-1938, I proudly entered second grade. It was a beautiful, cool September day and I was happy and felt so grown up. Mama walked me to school, wheeling Betty in her stroller with Charlotte holding on to one side of the handle bar, while I walked along, filled with excitement, clutching my brand-new pencil case and notebook. We walked the length of the Lange Kievitstraat, then through the tunnel under the railroad tracks that originated from the Antwerp Central Station and fanned out to many other destinations across Belgium. We exited the tunnel onto the Pelikaanstraat, turned left and headed to the Lamorinierestraat where the school was located. I would take this walk to school every day of the school year, but after that first day Mama would no longer accompany me. When I was safely delivered at school, Mama returned home with my younger sisters. They stayed home with her while Papa worked in his atelier.

At school we spoke Flemish, the language of the region, and at home we spoke Yiddish. I alternated automatically and easily between the two languages and used them interchangeably with my friends. I would walk to school alone or sometimes with some of my classmates, one of whom was my cousin's cousin, Heleneke, who was also my best friend.

The fall of 1937 flew by rapidly. In December we celebrated Hanukkah, our festival of light and freedom, by lighting Hanukkah candles for eight days, singing songs and playing dreidel. We also had a few days of vacation while the Christians celebrated Christmas and New Year, and went on outings to the center of the city to admire the lavish holiday displays in the department stores. We went to the Stadtpark to see if ice had formed on the lake and whether it was thick enough to skate on, but we were disappointed. Though it was cold and had snowed, there was no ice – and so we played and read at home, or visited with my friend Heleneke, Aunt Lea, Uncle Alex, and Nathan, who we called Nounou, our little cousin. Vacation ended all too soon and we all returned to our routines – mine was school, study and homework. But I did not fret. I enjoyed learning and was an avid reader.

One evening early in 1938, when my sisters and I were already in bed, I could hear Mama and Papa talking intensely; our bedroom was right next door to the dining room and it was easy to eavesdrop. I had just kissed them goodnight and left them sitting at the dining room table, which was still covered with empty dinner plates. There were "rumors" from Germany saying that it was dangerous to be Jewish. The Nazis who had been controlling Germany since 1933 were targeting Jewish men for persecution and were taking other anti-Jewish actions.

What I heard – though I did not completely understand it – shocked and frightened me, but I dared not get out of bed to ask them what it all meant. Continuing to listen, I learned that Mama feared that the German Nazis would encourage extremist groups in neighboring countries, including Belgium. I was frightened, but I was also very tired, and as I listened I must have fallen asleep. When I woke, it was morning and Mama and Papa had made a decision.

Papa would leave and try to get to America. Papa's sister, Sadie, lived in New York, and had urged him to come to the United States. Mama took over management of Papa's atelier while Papa worked as a ship's carpenter on a steamship for his one-way passage to America, which also allowed him to earn some money. Though told that the ship was headed for New York, where he planned to disembark, the ship instead sailed to Buenos Aires, Argentina.

We later learned that during the period between the World Wars, it was not unusual for steamship employers to lie to skilled craftsmen about their destinations, particularly when their services were especially needed.

Once you signed on, went aboard and the ship left the harbor, you had no choice, you were stuck, and forced to fulfill the obligations of the contract. Papa did his job during the lengthy journey and disembarked in Buenos Aires, where he tried to find another ship to take him to the United States, but to no avail. After several weeks, he found a captain who needed the skills of a good carpenter and returned him to Antwerp. We were delighted to have our Papa back with us because we had not expected to see him for a very long time.

But Mama was worried. The rumors and the news regarding Nazi Germany were getting worse. The Belgian population, Christian and Jewish alike, became more and more concerned. Papa continued to manage his atelier, while looking for a ship whose management he could trust to take him to the United States.

Papa went on his regular business trips to Mechelen (midway between Antwerp and Brussels) during that spring of 1938, and during the school holidays I accompanied him. I felt so privileged and grown up traveling alone with Papa on the train and was proud to be with him when he visited clients and shopped for catalogues showing the latest furniture styles.

After Papa had concluded his business, we stopped at a café for our midday meal before taking the train back to Antwerp. As we sat at a small table on the outdoor terrace of the café, I imagined the passersby looking at me with envy as I sat there proudly eating my lunch and talking to Papa. I felt so important! Then Papa treated me to my favorite dessert, dark chocolate ice cream. At that moment, I had no idea that this was the last time Papa and I would travel to Mechelen together and that when he left for America I would not see him again for eight-and-a-half long years. I also did not know that Mechelen, known as Malines in French, would become notorious as the city where the infamous Nazi transit camps for Jews were located or that many of my own aunts, uncles, cousins, and friends would be incarcerated there before being shipped to the Auschwitz-Birkenau concentration camp, never to return.

At Mama's urging, Papa intensified his efforts to get out of Europe. Papa finally found a Canadian ship that offered him work and travel to Canada. Since Canada shared a border with the United States, my parents felt it would be easier for Papa to contact his sister from Canada and then reach New York. It was even more difficult to say good-bye to Papa a second time, but we had to. Papa and Mama embraced and held each other for a long time. They apparently found it more difficult to part this time, too, since they had no idea when they would see each other again. Then Papa kissed each one of us and left.

Papa did make it to Canada and during 1939 emigrated to the U.S. and New York City. Life continued without Papa, just as it had when his first ship ended up in Argentina instead of the U.S. Mama worked in the atelier and took care of us. I sensed that a war had started, and Mama was nervous, but it didn't really affect me until May 1940, when I returned to Antwerp from the Fresh Air Camp at Oost Duinkerke. All the campers were sent home when it was announced that the Germans had invaded Belgium on May 10. Everyone in the city was on the run, Jew and Christian alike. Those who were old enough to remember World War I were afraid of a repetition of the brutality against the Belgians experienced during that war. Mama, whose demeanor was usually calm, was in a state of panic. I learned later that the invasion reminded her of the horrors of World War I she'd suffered as a six-year-old in her native Romania.

Chaos reigned in the city. People were in the streets loading bicycles, horse-drawn wagons, cars, baby carriages, strollers, and running somewhere. People just wanted to put as great a distance as possible between themselves and the tanks – those ominous German tanks.

Our neighbor, Shimon, had a car and was preparing to leave with his family. He suggested we join them and offered us the trundle seat, a seat that jutted from the back of the car where the trunk was usually located.

Mama packed the necessities we needed for our unexpected journey while I placed the items I wanted to take on the table near the open suitcases. I put my violin and my doll on the table.

"No, no, Flora, not the violin. We're not taking the violin." she admonished me gently.

"Why not?" I asked.

"Because a violin will likely identify us as Jews," she answered.

I was puzzled. Why would owning a violin be a sign that we were Jewish? Many people played the violin. Not all violinists were Jewish. And besides, what was wrong with being Jewish? At the time, I never had any experience with specific antisemitism; I did not understand the meaning of what she was saying. I'd heard Mama, Aunt Lea, and other family members talk about the antisemitism prevalent in the countries of their birth and why they came to live in Belgium, the beautiful country of my birth.

Belgium had a reputation for tolerance. I was so proud to be Belgian. I did not know then that I was not a Belgian, though I was born in a suburb of Antwerp. I did not learn until after World War II that, according to Belgian law, I was Romanian, a citizen of the country of my parents' birth. I also had difficulty understanding the full meaning of the term *antisemitism*. True, some of the children in school called me "The Jewish girl with the curly hair." Though I didn't like it, I never thought of it as antisemitism.

Mama told Shimon that Charlotte was still not home from the Fresh Air Camp at Heist-Aan-Zee and that we had to wait for her. Mama tried to contact the camp but could not reach anyone. However, she was certain that since I had come back, Charlotte would return shortly. She asked Shimon to wait until her return. Mama assured him that it would not be long. He expressed his willingness to wait. However, his wife was not because she feared for the safety of her children. Nevertheless, they agreed to wait. Several hours passed and Charlotte had not come back. Finally, Shimon told us he and his family could wait no longer, that they were leaving whether we went with them or not. Mama decided to go, taking Betty and me.

Our friends, the Pollacks – Benjamin, Fanny, and their seven-year-old son Harry – lived across the street from us on the Lange Kievitstraat. They decided not to flee, based on the premise that people panic too quickly and make wrong decisions because of haste and fear. They risked staying at home, with the hope that everything would turn out well. Mama asked them to look out for Charlotte, to please take her in when she came home from camp and that we would come back for her. It was a decision that left Mama guilt-stricken the rest of her life. She told me many years later, when I was an adult with children of my own, that she had uncharacteristically panicked during the German invasion. Looking back after all the intervening years, she realized that at the time she had not been thinking clearly and had acted hastily when she decided to leave Charlotte behind, hoping she would be safe with the Pollacks.

While Shimon and his family settled into his car, Mama helped me climb into the trundle seat. I held the doll Mama had recently bought me. She was wearing a beautiful rose-colored woolen dress Mama had knitted for her, with a pretty hat, topped with a big pompom that Mama had crocheted. I still could not understand why Mama would not permit me to take my violin. As I was settling into the seat I continued to question Mama.

"Mama, are you sure I can't take my violin? I won't be able to practice if I don't have my violin. I'll forget how to play and my teacher will be angry," I argued.

"It's all right; you'll make up for it later by practicing more," she replied emphatically, and ended the discussion.

Mama placed Betty on my lap, and I held her as best as I could to make her comfortable, but she had the measles and her body felt hot and feverish. Then she put her little head against my shoulder and moaned. Mama placed our three small suitcases and the bag containing food and a bottle of milk for Betty on the floor near my feet and climbed into the trundle seat next to me. She took the baby from me and placed her on her own lap, where Betty soon fell asleep, her little legs draped over mine. Mama's coat served as a blanket and covered her.

Shimon turned the ignition key to start the engine and we left Antwerp without Charlotte and without my violin. I couldn't stop thinking about both, but as much as I loved my violin, my thoughts were with my little sister.

"Mommy, are we leaving without Charlotte? How will Charlotte know where we are? Why don't we wait for her?" Mama replied that Charlotte would be fine with the Pollack family until we returned. But I kept thinking how upset she was going to be when she came back from camp and did not find us at home.

Although it was May, the weather on this particular day was cold and windy. While Shimon and his family were sitting in the comfort of the closed car, we sat in the open trundle seat. As we rode, I played with my doll. A sudden gust of wind pulled the doll from my hands, and the doll flew out of the car onto the road. I started to cry.

Mama knocked on the back window of the car, motioning for Shimon to stop so we could try to retrieve the doll. He refused. After all, we were not exactly on a pleasure ride. We were trying to escape from the enemy. Even if he had tried to stop, he would not have been able to do so without causing other drivers, also fleeing from the German onslaught, to become very angry. The road, both in front of us and behind us, was crowded with vehicles of all types – cars, motorcycles, bicycles and wagons pulled by horses. In addition, the road was filled with people on foot, some pushing baby carriages that held babies and luggage. Others were pushing strollers with toddlers in them, and yet others were walking, weighed down with backpacks and suitcases. The sides of the road were packed with people sitting or lying on the ground, trying to rest for a while before continuing on their journey of escape from the invading Germans.

Thus we continued on our way without stopping to retrieve my doll, my precious doll, which by now was probably already crushed to a pulp by the wheels of the other vehicles behind us. My tears flowed as I mourned the loss of my cherished doll.

Suddenly, the car started to make a strange grinding noise, slowed down and rolled to a halt. Shimon got out and lifted the hood to find the source of the problem. People behind us started honking their car horns. The noise was deafening. Everyone was tense. Shimon found nothing visibly wrong with the motor. Then he checked the fuel gauge. The tank was empty. In his rush to leave Antwerp he had forgotten to check. What to do now? There were no petrol stations. We were in a quandary.

The only solution was to abandon the car and continue on foot like the many others on the road. All of us, except Mama, who held Betty, got behind the car and pushed it to the side of the road. We were accompanied by loud angry shouts from people hanging out the windows of their vehicles. The noise of the honking horns and the arms of people in cars waving angrily for us to get out of their way made us anxious.

After a short discussion, Shimon, his wife and Mama decided that under the circumstances it would be better for each family to continue separately. We took whatever luggage we could carry, wished each other good luck, and continued on our separate ways by foot. Mama carried Betty and the bag of food and I carried two suitcases – we left one in the abandoned car. We had no idea where we were at this point, but we knew that we had not yet crossed the border into France. We soon learned that we were close to the border, but were still in Belgium.

CHAPTER 2

France

We walked and walked and rested at the side of the road with all the other refugees. And then we walked some more. At night, we slept in the fields, huddled together under Mama's coat. Occasionally, a kind farmer would allow us to sleep in his barn and give us some fresh milk for Betty, for which we were very grateful. Fortunately, it didn't rain, and we continued on our way for several days.

When we came to the border with northern France, the border guards checked people's documents carefully. Some people were turned back because anyone without an identity card or a passport showing legal residence in a Western European country was not permitted to cross. Mama's identity card showed her legal residence in Belgium, so we were allowed through and continued our journey on foot. Vans bearing the well-known Red Cross symbol, stationed at different spots alongside the road, distributed food and beverages to the masses of refugees, including the three of us. I remember being given some lemonade and a few cookies. The Red Cross workers also gave people balm and bandages for the blisters and sores on their feet, and it seemed everyone appreciated what they were doing for us. I saw Mama thank them profusely when they gave her milk for Betty.

As we walked, I began to notice Belgian and French soldiers retreating from the German invading forces that were getting closer to the Belgian-French border. The soldiers looked pitiful – unshaven, in dirty uniforms, looking terribly tired – as if they hadn't slept in days. Even in our own difficult circumstances, Mama and I felt sorry for them.

We entered Calais, a busy port city on the Manche, the English Channel, approximately one hundred thirty miles from Antwerp. It was late afternoon; I think it may have been about six days after we fled Antwerp, around May 18 or 19, 1940. We were trying to find a place to spend the night when the shriek of air raid sirens pierced the sky. Everyone on the street ran into bomb shelters; we followed the crowd. Packed in, most of the people in the shelter had to stand because the benches along the walls were filled. Two kind people offered us their seats when they saw how tired we were and how ill Betty was. She still felt quite hot and feverish to the touch, but we had no thermometer to check her temperature. All we could do was sit in the dim, crowded space and wait for the all clear signal.

Once it sounded, I could hear people sigh with relief and then begin to file out of the shelter. Mama told me to remain with Betty until she came back; she wanted to try to find us some lodgings and we could rest in the shelter until she returned. I don't remember how long I sat there with Betty, but we were alone. I had always been afraid of the dark and now I was really frightened. Betty moaned and cried that she was thirsty, but I had nothing to give her to drink.

After what seemed like an eternity, I decided to disobey Mama's order and leave. I picked up Betty, holding her with one arm, and with the other, I picked up and carried one of the suitcases and the bag of food. I could not carry the second suitcase so I left it behind, figuring that when I found Mama we could come back and get it.

Betty, holding on to her teddy bear, draped her arms around my neck. When we exited into the street it was pitch dark. There were no streetlights, no light coming from the black-shaded house windows, and no stars to light our way." Mama! Mama! Mama!" I called as I walked. Poor Betty felt very heavy in my arms. She was so ill, feverish and hot and I didn't know what to do. Mama had gone away in this strange city, and I couldn't find her. I walked and cried as loud as I could, "Mama, Mama, Mama!"

Mama had not been able to find lodgings, and when she tried to make her way back to the bomb shelter in the blackness of the night, she had lost her way. As I walked and shouted, I heard a voice shouting, "Floreke, Floreke!" I shouted even louder and we found each other. Mama hugged both of us and sobbed," My babies, my babies…"

We then began walking together, not really knowing where we were going. Mama carried Betty and I carried the suitcase. Mama seemed to have completely forgotten about the second suitcase, and we never went back to the bomb shelter to retrieve it.

By then, the sky had cleared and stars had made their appearance, somewhat lighting our way. Soon we found ourselves at the Calais harbor, where there was lots of activity. A large ship bearing a Red Cross flag was in the dock and men in uniform were scurrying back and forth, carrying stretchers up the gangplank.

Mama approached one of the men who looked like an officer and asked about the ship. She learned that they were taking wounded soldiers to England for medical care and animatedly started telling him that her husband was in the United States and that she would be grateful if they could take us with them to England. She also offered to help with the wounded in return for our passage.

Had she forgotten about Charlotte? She had not. When the officer left his post to inquire about Mama's request, she explained her plans to me. If we got passage to England, she would contact the Pollack family in Antwerp to find out if they had Charlotte and also contact Papa in the States. Then she would find a way to bring Charlotte either to England or directly to America, if we managed to get there. It was a fantasy, but under the unreal circumstances in which we found ourselves, Mama apparently did not realize this. The officer returned. He told Mama to wait and, if there was space left after all the wounded were aboard, he would consider taking us.

We sat down to wait. Mama sat on the suitcase, holding Betty, and I sat on the concrete floor of the quay at her side, resting my head against her arm. We waited. The night turned into dawn and still we waited. Finally, the officer with whom Mama had spoken earlier approached us. He hesitated for a moment, handed Mama a small bag containing a few cookies, then told her it was impossible to take us aboard, that he was very sorry. He returned to the ship, went up the gangplank, which was then lifted, and the ship slowly made its way out of the harbor.

Now what? We continued walking alongside the harbor and thought about leaving Calais to try to reach Switzerland. We saw a crowd of people boarding what looked like a fishing vessel and asked them about the boat. No one knew to whom it belonged, but one of the refugees was familiar with fishing boats and knew how to steer one. He was encouraged by the other refugees to take charge of this apparently abandoned vessel. We all climbed aboard, and Mama found us a small space to sit on deck with our backs against the cabin wall. We made ourselves as comfortable as possible and put Betty, who was still not feeling too well, across both our laps so she could rest and sleep.

The fishing vessel was fully loaded with every bit of space filled with refugees. Suddenly, someone, possibly the owner of the boat, came running and shouting that the vessel was not operational, that it was waiting to be taken away for repairs. As the man shouted, the boat tipped on its side, plunging half the people into the water. Mama, Betty and I were fortunate. The cabin wall against which we had been leaning was now under us and we now sat on it instead of against it, keeping us somewhat dry.

Men on the quay came running toward the boat and threw life preservers and rope ladders into the sea to help those in the water and those of us still on the overturned boat to climb to the safety of the quay. Several men climbed down the rope ladders and lifted the children, taking them up to safety – thus were we rescued.

Somehow our only remaining suitcase, containing the few items of clothing we still had left, was also rescued, but we had to revise our escape plans. After a few minutes rest, we followed another crowd of refugees, without knowing where we were heading. We were very tired and barely cared. All we wanted was a place to rest. By this time, we no longer kept track of what day of the week it was, or even the date.

After walking and following the crowd for about an hour, we arrived at the Calais railroad station and entered the terminal building. There, in the center, was a table manned by Red Cross workers who were distributing food and drinks to the refugees. The cookies we'd gotten from the Marine at the harbor were long gone. As tired, hungry and thirsty as we were, it was a welcome sight. We joined the queue and, like everyone else, patiently waited our turn. After a long wait we were given some food and something to drink, and then made our way through the crowd to an empty corner. We sat down on the floor and used the suitcase as a table. Though we were extremely tired, we enjoyed every bite and sip. Even Betty ate.

We spent most of the night in that corner of the railway station, dozing fitfully but we were not the only ones sleeping on the floor that night. All across the terminal, groups of people were also trying to rest and sleep.

Railroad employees walked around shuffling people here and there to keep the paths open, but were very considerate of those resting.

The next morning we tried to purchase train tickets. Mama, after hesitating for a while and thinking out loud of perhaps trying to return to Belgium to fetch Charlotte, realized that this was impossible. So we tried to get tickets to Switzerland in our attempt get to America and then send for Charlotte. But the ticket windows were closed. People headed for the train tracks without tickets and boarded trains without worrying about the destination. We saw people heading for a train that was supposedly traveling south, so we decided to get on it. It wasn't easy. People pushed their way on. The bigger and stronger ones elbowed their way ahead of the smaller and weaker among us. None of them cared if they injured others or not. All they wanted to do was get on that train. Nothing else mattered. I wondered what happened to the nice patient people in the previous evening's queue. When the train left, the three of us were left standing on the platform wondering what to do next. We went back into the main terminal with me still carrying our lone suitcase.

Then we learned that the train we couldn't board was the last train to leave Calais and that no other trains would service the station. The Red Cross workers gave us some more food and something to drink and we spent another day and night in our little corner, dozing off and on.

The next morning we left the terminal without the suitcase. It had simply become too heavy for either of us to continue carrying it and Mama still had to carry Betty. I took the cloth grocery bag containing our last few necessities and slung it over my shoulder. We walked, as we had for days, following other refugees, but now we could hear the increasingly frequent sounds of shooting behind us, and realized the German ground forces were pushing further and further into France. They were not far behind, forcing us to continue moving forward.

We walked south for about four or five more days before we arrived at the outskirts of Boulogne-sur-Mer. We were very tired, so as we had often done before, we sat down on the side of the road to rest for a while. Complaining about being tired had become a daily litany. I would start by complaining, then Mama would respond that she was tired, too, and Betty would end it by whining about being tired. As we sat there, suddenly Mama started to cry, tears running down her cheeks, mumbling her regrets at having left Charlotte behind. "I shouldn't have. Why did I leave her behind? What possessed me?

Why did I? Why did I not wait for my Charlotte? Why did I not...? Floreke, do you think she's safe? Do you think we'll find her again?"

I didn't answer. I just looked at her sad, forlorn face. I didn't like it when Mama was sad. I needed her.

Then Mama made new plans. She decided that we must go back to Antwerp to find Charlotte. We could not and would not continue on our journey without her, all four of us had to be together.

But that was easier said than done.

Heading back would be more difficult than going forward – it would be like pushing against the tide. It was June, and the roads were still packed with refugees. In addition, there were troops fleeing from the advancing German Army, and we learned that the Germans by then had already conquered most of northern France. The situation was chaotic. We were literally being forced forward by the crowd; there could be no turning back. Entering Boulogne-sur-Mer, and because we were so exhausted, Mama decided to find us a place to sleep. She planned to have us spend a few days recuperating before venturing forth again.

Mama entered several shops to inquire about lodgings. At first she was not successful because the city was so crowded with refugees that beds were scarce. Then she spotted a small, clean-looking café and went in to ask. Fortune smiled upon us, for the kind proprietress, Mme. Martines, offered us lodgings at her home. The café was on the street level of the building she lived in and owned. The apartments were on the upper two floors, and she gave us a comfortable bedroom with an adjoining kitchenette. Mme. Martines refused to take any money as payment for our lodgings and food, so Mama offered to help her in the café.

Soon after we settled in, German troops entered Boulogne-sur-Mer and were visible on all the streets of the city. To protest, Mme. Martines closed her café so she would not have to serve the German troops – those *"sales boches"* (dirty Germans), as she called them. However, the "new" police soon ordered her to reopen and serve every paying customer.

While Mama and Mme. Martines worked, Betty and I roamed the streets of the city. Betty was feeling well by then and had turned four years old on June 7.

One sunny morning, as Betty and I window shopped, we noticed a crowd of people in front of some stores that had their front glass display windows and doors broken. People were looting; barging into the stores and running out with arms loaded with merchandise – shoes, boots, purses, coats. I thought the windows were probably broken during the last air raid and decided that I could push our way into the shop that displayed a pair of white rain boots and a raincoat I had previously admired during one of our walks. Betty and I grabbed whatever we could and, with arms loaded, ran as fast as we could back to the café. I had what I wanted, the white boots and raincoat.

But Mama was very angry. She scolded me: "You are the oldest, and as the oldest you should have set a better example for your younger sister!" She took the items she said we had stolen away from us and told us she planned to return them to the owner of the shop as soon as she had some free time. Betty and I followed Mama upstairs to the room the three of us shared and watched as she placed the items under the bed and reiterated that they would be returned to their proper owner. I was upset and angry. Though I knew very well what I had done was wrong, I argued: "I was not the only one who took things from the shop. Many others did also, and they were grown-ups."

I also knew that once Mama decided to do something, she did it. I would not be able to keep those boots and the coat. A few days went by and Mama still had not returned the items to the store. Meanwhile, I kept praying for rain, as I was anxious to wear the raincoat and especially the boots at least once – I knew that otherwise Mama would not relent. I kept hoping she would change her mind and allow me to keep the raincoat and beautiful boots that I loved so much. For several days after the looting incident, there was still no rain.

So a few days later, on a bright sunny day, while Mama was working in the café and Betty was with her, I quietly retrieved the boots and the raincoat from under the bed and slipped out of the house without being seen. Once outside, I sat down on the doorstep and put on the boots and raincoat. I walked proudly through the sunny streets of Boulogne-sur-Mer feeling very elegant. Unfortunately, I thoughtlessly walked past the shop from which I had taken the boots and raincoat and suddenly felt myself being lifted from the back by the collar. I turned and faced an angry man, the owner of the shop. He screamed at me, called me a thief, and threatened to have me arrested. He made me remove the raincoat and boots right then and there in the middle of the street. Many passersby stopped and looked at us and smiled. Apparently they found the scene entertaining.

I, on the other hand, was terribly humiliated. As soon as the owner released me, I ran back, barefoot, to our lodgings as quickly as I could. Mama reprimanded me severely and did not allow me to go outdoors for two whole days. When my punishment was lifted, I had to promise to always obey her orders. She said that everything she did or told me to do was because she loved me.

As she uttered those words, her eyes filled with tears. She started again to mutter in a tremulous voice: "Why didn't I? Why didn't I? Why didn't I wait for Charlotte to return before leaving? God only knows where she is ..." My eyes also filled with tears. I had great difficulty watching Mama cry. I went over to her, put my arms around her waist and my head against her body and tried to console her. Mama tried to think of some way to contact the Pollacks in Antwerp in order to find out if Charlotte was with them, but that was impossible.

Several weeks passed. Mama worked in the café with Mme. Martines and I took care of Betty. Life during our stay became almost routine: Mama worked, Betty and I played, and I had the added responsibility of watching over my little sister. By now we were used to seeing the German soldiers in Mme. Martines' café and in the streets. But our days and nights alternated between periods of quiet and air raids. When the ear-splitting sirens went off, we all ran to the shelters. Then it would become quiet again for a day or two.

Toward the middle of June, Mama decided that instead of trying to get to Switzerland and then trying to find transportation to America, she would first try to find people in France willing to take Betty and me into their home for a while. Then she would attempt to make her way back to Antwerp, find Charlotte, and bring her back to France. Then all four of us would try to make our way to Switzerland, America and to Papa. Unfortunately by the time she was ready to execute her new plan, we learned that the Swiss had closed the borders to prevent refugees, especially Jewish refugees, from entering their land.

CHAPTER 3

Orders to Return

In July, The German occupiers posted orders instructing all those who had recently entered France from other countries and those who were not legal residents to return to the countries from which they came. We said goodbye to Mme. Martines, our wonderful hostess, who so kindly had sheltered us for six weeks. She insisted on giving Mama some money that she claimed Mama had earned by working during our stay. Mama tried to refuse to take the gift, but Mme. Martines insisted that Mama had earned it. When Mama then tried to pay her for our room and board, she refused to accept it.

We said our goodbyes and began our journey back to Antwerp.

Mama and I wondered what had ever happened to Shimon and his family. We never saw them again and never learned their fate. We traveled for several days, taking short train rides between the towns where the tracks had not been damaged. We walked and even hitchhiked with German soldiers, as strange as that may seem. When we were offered rides by German soldiers we were careful to pretend that we did not understand them. Even I knew it was not safe, lest the soldiers think we were Jews. Mama kept repeating in French, *"Belgique, Belgique, Anvers, Anvers…"*

It was strange coming back home after all those weeks away. When we finally arrived at our home in Antwerp, we thankfully found the apartment intact; surprisingly, no one had broken in. Charlotte was safe and well with the Pollack family, and she was excited and happy to see us, but she was also very angry with Mama. Her anger was mixed with the fear of having been abandoned by her family. If I had been the one who had been left behind, I would probably have been just as angry and afraid. We'd left Antwerp in the middle of May and it was now the middle of July. That was a long time for a seven-year-old to be away from her family, especially in wartime.

I was reunited with many of my cherished possessions. The first thing I looked for was my beloved violin. I saw the case in the exact place where I had left it. When I opened it, the violin was lying there safely, together with my bow. I was relieved to have my precious violin, and I now would be able to practice and be prepared for my lessons when my teacher returned. But my teacher, who had fled Antwerp when the invasion began, never came back and I never learned what happened to him.

Occasionally I could still hear Mama murmuring to herself about leaving Charlotte behind. She would talk to herself, but loudly enough for me to hear. "I don't know, I don't understand how I could have done this, I don't know...."

The four of us settled back into our apartment, returning to what I thought would be a somewhat normal life, but I was wrong. The streets were filled with German men in uniform, ordinary soldiers and officers. We covered our windows with blackout shades to prevent light from being seen from outside, to prevent planes from spotting the city from above.

At first, things felt normal. I was happy with my toys, books, and my miniature porcelain tea set, but I missed my favorite doll, the one the wind had ripped from my hands as we sat in the trundle seat of Shimon's car. We found two of the several teddy bears we shared. Mama instructed me to give one to Betty and one to Charlotte, who was also reunited with some of her favorite toys.

All of this was fine, but survival became of vital importance. Finding food for us became Mama's urgent priority, and she succeeded by becoming a seamstress to earn enough money to buy food and pay the rent. She took the time to teach me how to sew, and took extra time for a special lesson on how to sew on buttons.

Slowly many family members, friends and neighbors drifted back from the many places to which they had fled when the German Army *blitzkreiged* Belgium and France. I was especially happy when my favorite uncle, Uncle Alex, returned with Aunt Lea, Mama's youngest sister, and their little boy, Nounou. They settled back into their apartment on Terlis Straat. Uncle Alex's sister, Rachel, her husband, Muniek, and their children, Heleneke – who was my best friend – and Louis also came home.

Uncle Alex's other sister, Chany, and her husband, Mendel, were also back in Antwerp with their two sons, Jackie and two-year-old Henry, whom we called Harreke. Jackie was my idol. He was four years older than me, and he didn't know it, but I planned on marrying him as soon as I grew up.

Despite air raids, blackouts and the German soldiers, life during the month of August – when I celebrated my tenth birthday – took on a semblance of prewar routine. On Friday evenings, behind the blackout shades, Mama again lit Sabbath candles and recited the blessing over them. Yet I no longer felt the joy I used to feel when I would look at the candles' flickering flames before that terrible day, May 10.

Somehow, on Friday evenings, when we were bringing in the Sabbath, Papa's absence was felt most poignantly. During the weekly Sabbath meal, Mama would sadly utter her oft repeated question: "Why can't Papa be with us, instead of being so far away in America? I should have never let him leave by himself. Who knows when we'll see him again? It is too difficult to carry the whole burden of taking care of the children by myself in these trying times."

Her eyes would fill with tears, and I would rise from my chair, go to her, put my arms around her, and tell her that I would be good, that I would help her take care of my sisters so that things would not be so difficult for her. Mama would then wipe her tears while I walked back to my seat and we'd all finish the meal in silence. It was at times like this that I missed Papa even more.

We resumed our weekly Sunday family outings to the Antwerp Stadt-park (City Park) at the end of the Lange Kievistraat. We rode our bicycles, just like we'd done before the invasion, with Betty sitting in the special rear seat on Mama's bicycle. We enjoyed our midday picnics in the park with our extended family members and friends and took pleasure looking at the grace-ful swans gliding on the lake and in playing games.

We once again sang our favorite songs, like *Ochy Czarny* (Dark Eyes), to the accompaniment of the music Uncle Alex's fingers drew from the strings of his mandolin – an instrument he taught me to play. I was always fascinated to see and hear how music could be drawn from two string instruments and sound quite different from each other. The violin required me to use my fingers and the bow to bring forth a melody, whereas the music of the mandolin was brought forth by just a pick and the player's fingers. At these get-togethers, I would wonder about what could have happened to my music teacher.

At the beginning of September, as we had done every year prior to 1940, we returned to school and adjusted ourselves to the familiar routine of attending classes, doing homework, taking exams, and so forth. But while all these activities were familiar and normal, several things changed. In October, Jews had to register so that the governing powers knew who was Christian and who was Jewish. Many people did not register, but Mama and the other members of the family reluctantly did. They did not really have much choice. If they did not register, they would not receive the special food ration card every person needed in order to get the monthly allotment of food stamps – after all, everyone had to eat. Then a curfew was imposed from 8 p.m. to 7 a.m.

Even with the food stamps, finding enough food became a daily ordeal. Because Mama worked, it was my responsibility to buy the groceries after school. I dreaded that chore, but I was the eldest and thus had no choice. There was always a long queue waiting to enter the grocery store. Because I was much smaller than the adults, they often pushed me back by swinging their arms back and forth at me or by kicking me so they could jump the line. Often, by the time I got inside, the grocery store would be empty. Even when I was able to purchase groceries, there was never enough to satiate our hunger.

Most people, especially those in the cities, never had enough food to satisfy their hunger. Those with a good supply of cash could buy additional food from the flourishing black market. However, by 1941, Jewish bank accounts were frozen so Jews could no longer withdraw any of the savings. Jewish employees were dismissed from their jobs. Because they had to hang signs on their stores identifying them as Jewish-owned businesses, Jewish shop owners lost much income because of the loss of their clientele.

During a meeting on October 10, 1940, General von Falkenhausen, the German Military Commander for Belgium and northern France, informed Belgian civil government leaders of the anti-Jewish decrees that the occupiers planned to implement. The Belgian leaders told him that under the Belgian Constitution all Belgians were equal under the law and entitled to general and public employment regardless of their birth, religious or political affiliation.

Regardless, Jewish government employees were dismissed on orders from the German rulers. The Belgian government tried to resist for a while, but finally felt it had no choice. The occupiers were in control.

The situation for the Jewish residents of Antwerp continued to deteriorate. Everyone over the age of fifteen had to carry an identity card that showed the bearer's name, address, profession, date of birth, place of birth, and nationality. Mama's identity card was yellow, with a red band running across the three outer pages which bore the words *Etranger* and *Vreemdeling* ("foreigner" in French and Flemish), because Mama was not born in Belgium. She was from Romania. And Mama's card – like that of all the other Jews – was stamped with the words *Juif* and *Jood* ("Jew" in French and Flemish) in red on the front page. Belgian citizens carried green cards without any bands of another color running across them.

This was the beginning of the real sustained reign of terror against the Jewish people. We were then deprived of food ration cards and obtaining food became a major problem. German authorities began implementing other debilitating actions as well. Jewish people lost their jobs. Jewish-owned bank accounts, securities and properties were confiscated by the German occupiers. Jewish places of business were still allowed to operate, but had to display a notice on their windows or doors identifying them as Jewish-owned enterprises.

Soon after the Germans occupied Belgium and France, they ordered the Belgians who fled to return, especially the Jewish residents of Antwerp, many of whom worked in the diamond industry. For a short time, exceptions from the new laws were made for these workers because the enemy needed their expertise. The occupiers especially needed diamond cutters, so they had promised that no harm would befall the workers who were needed for the war effort.

The Germans issued other orders. The one that directed people to give up their radios made Mama particularly unhappy because we were no longer able to listen to the news. The radio news we had been hearing had already been censored by the German authorities, so we couldn't understand the new rule. Some people managed to keep special hidden radios that allowed them to listen to clandestine programs and news.

We were still able to listen to music from Mama's extensive record collection as long as we played it softly so no one outside our apartment could hear it. Many of those were recordings of classical and Yiddish music. Life gradually became more and more difficult for those of us who were Jewish.

Soon our food ration cards became invalid, making life even harder for us. It was no longer possible to buy any food from regular grocery shops, forcing more and more Jews to turn to the black market.

By 1941, Mama became a smuggler and began bringing food in from Lille in northern France, where it was more easily obtainable. Some she sold on the black market and some she kept for the four of us. With the money from food sales we were able to buy perishables like milk and eggs, and occasionally, some vegetables and fruit. When Mama went on her smuggling trips, I cared for my two younger sisters – quite a responsibility for a ten-year-old.

It was my job to wake my sisters early each morning and prepare breakfast for all three of us. After we ate, we cleaned the apartment before we walked to school, which was on Lamoriniere Straat, quite a distance from our home. In Antwerp during those years, there were no school buses. If transportation was needed, parents would usually accompany their young children on the tram.

After school, we would walk home, where I would serve a snack and help Charlotte with her homework while Betty played at our side. Then I would do my homework. In exchange for some food, one of our neighbors, Magda, a single woman, would look in on us, but mostly we were alone. Occasionally, if a neighbor was willing to watch my sisters for a few days, I would cut school and accompany Mama to France to help with the smuggling. According to Mama, children were not easily suspected or as carefully scrutinized as adults, and we could bring more food back because I could help her carry the packages.

I didn't always go with her because my teachers would have become suspicious if I were absent too often. Besides, Mama needed me to stay with my sisters because there was a limit as to how often she could ask Magda to take charge of Betty and Charlotte.

Whenever Mama left on her trips I feared that she might be arrested and that I would not see her again, so I waited for her return impatiently. I missed her, as did my sisters, and fortunately, she always came home safely. As time passed, however, it became more difficult to cross into France. Border guards asked travelers why they were visiting France and became increasingly suspicious of people coming in from Belgium.

Sometimes we would take the train to Lille, one of the first cities just over the Belgian-French border. We would leave the train at the last stop on the Belgian side of the border and stay in the neighborhood until night fell. As soon as it would get dark we would cross the border into France from a lightly guarded area on the Belgian side. Once we were safely on the French side, we would rest behind some bushes and wait for daylight. When the sun made its appearance, we would walk nonchalantly to the nearest bus stop and board a bus to the center of Lille. There, we would make our way to a small café and inn where Mama knew the owner, a man called Josef. He permitted us to use the café to meet the locals who sold us food and other items.

We always spent the night in Lille before we went back to Antwerp because by the time we made our purchases, it was too late to cross the border back into Belgium and catch the train to Antwerp. We also needed to find people to take the merchandise across the border for us. Usually, that would be a German soldier in the Wehrmacht – and we always had to be careful and pick men who wore the correct uniforms of the regular German army.

The truth is that even German soldiers were generally willing to help a woman with a child. Often, soldiers far away from home, who perhaps were longing for their families, would engage a local child in conversation by smiling and offering a sweet – like a piece of candy or a cookie. So Mama and I developed a system. When a soldier offered me candy, I would smile back and then Mama, who was always close by, would join the conversation. The soldier, learning that we were not residents of Lille, would ask why we were there. Mama would say she was the sole caretaker of her three children and that her husband, a Belgian soldier, was a prisoner of war and we were in Lille to bring back needed food for the family because there was no food in Antwerp. Somehow this always evoked sympathy and the soldiers usually, but not always, generously offered to help us take the groceries across the border.

When we were unable to obtain help, we had to attempt to cross and pass through customs by ourselves. On one such trip to Lille, we brought with us the empty doll box for my doll I had lost when we tried to escape the invasion the previous year. In Lille, we filled this box with sugar and tried and failed to find someone to help us bring it across to Belgium, so we had to smuggle it in ourselves. As we attempted to go through the open gate to Belgium, a customs agent approached us. Mama was carrying a bag filled with several loaves of bread that were promptly confiscated and I was carrying the box of sugar. The bread was a ploy – because we thought that after they took the bread away from Mama they would not search any further. Mama had also hidden inside her garments some wool fabric that, if we could safely get it to Antwerp, would sell for a handsome sum that would keep us in food for at least a week.

After he took Mama's bread, the customs agent turned to me and reached for the doll's box. I started to scream: "Mama, Mama, the man wants to take my box away! He wants to take my doll!" I held the box closely to my chest and tried to turn away from the customs agent as he was reaching for it.

I cried even louder: "Mama, don't let him take my doll, he'll break it, he'll break my new doll!" He tried again, surprisingly gentle, "I only want to look at her, little one, I won't hurt her, I promise." But I did not cease screaming until he finally said, in a voice that sounded more tired than annoyed, "Okay, okay, don't be afraid. Keep your doll, I won't touch it." With that, he waved us on.

Of course, we were delighted, but did not show it until we were safely back in Antwerp and could relax and tell the story to some family members and friends. My sisters were happy to have us back home and our success meant we would have a variety of foods to eat for a few weeks. Magda, the unmarried neighbor who cared for Charlotte and Betty while we were gone, was also happy because she got her fair share of the food in exchange for minding the girls.

By 1942, life at school became increasingly difficult and unpleasant. The non-Jewish pupils teased me and called me and the other Jewish students nasty names. They also pushed us and "accidentally" bumped into us. The teachers were too intimidated to reprimand the perpetrators because they weren't sure whose parents might be members of one of the antisemitic groups collaborating with the Nazi regime.

My sister and I, along with the other Jewish children in school, didn't have to suffer the taunts of the other pupils for too long. Soon an order was issued that prohibited Jewish children from attending the public schools. The only school we were allowed to attend was the Jewish Day School, and that is where most parents enrolled their children.

But Mama did not register us. I asked her why. She said that she was not sure, but she had a *feeling* it was not a good idea. This was a very wise decision, as we later learned.

Then, as of May 1942 all Jews, including children, had to wear a yellow patch in the shape of a Jewish star on their clothes to identify them when they went out on the street or to any public place. I hated wearing that star, but now that I no longer went to school, I accompanied Mama more often on her smuggling trips to Lille. I liked going on those trips despite the difficulties and the risk because I liked being with Mama by myself. On our trips to Lille, I did not have to share her with anyone. She was all mine and I received all her attention.

A short time later, our food smuggling trips came to an abrupt halt. Mama and I no longer went to Lille, nor did Mama go by herself. Once in a while, when I'd ask if we would ever go to Lille again, she simply said, "No." She never explained, or gave me any reason.

I accepted that reply from Mama because I somehow knew instinctively when not to press for explanations. But her answer troubled me. Although Mama never explained it, I realized much later that what had happened during our last evening in Lille probably ended our smuggling trips, though I was not aware of it at that time. It was a Thursday and Mama wanted us to return the next morning, on Friday. She always wanted to be home in time to light the Sabbath candles, if possible.

As usual, when we arrived at the café, we were warmly greeted by Josef and had supper. He always offered us nice large portions even though we had no food ration stamps. Afterward, we chatted with some of the regular patrons who knew us, and proceeded to make connections to purchase merchandise and arrange to cross the border with our provisions in the morning.

While we were eating, a group of German officers entered the café, sat down, ordered food and wine, looked at me and smiled. I smiled back and one of the officers said something. Though I understood what he said, as per Mama's instructions, I made a facial expression indicating my lack of comprehension. The officer then called someone over who could interpret in French and Flemish. We connected. He moved over to our table and continued to talk to us, mostly to Mama, via the interpreter. Mama related her usual story that she was alone and had to feed three young children and that her husband, a Belgian soldier, was a prisoner of war. He agreed to carry our provisions over the border for us the following day. After a polite period of time we said goodnight and went down to our room, one floor below the street level of the café.

As we prepared for bed, there was a knock at the door. Mama asked who it was, and it was the officer we had just left in the café. Mama said to him in French, *"Demain,"* meaning tomorrow. He knocked again, this time much harder than before. Mama opened the door slightly and politely told him to go away, avoiding the German language. He understood and got angry. As she tried to close the door again, he pushed it open forcefully and walked into the room. He picked me up from the bed, took me to the staircase landing outside our room, plunked me down in the corner, and motioned for me with a threatening face not to move from there.

He went back into our room, but before he could close the door, I got up and reentered the room. He made threatening motions toward me, pointing to the door with an outstretched arm. Mama moved toward me and placed herself between him and me in order to protect me. He forcefully pushed her back. He was tall and much stronger than either Mama or I. Mama was only five feet tall and I was a small eleven-year-old. He picked me up again, took me out of the room, and again plunked me down in the corner of the landing with such force that my buttocks hurt for days.

I don't know how long I sat there, frightened, trembling and cold. I could not understand why I was forbidden to be in the room with Mama. Why was that man, who had been so nice and kind when we first met him in the dining area of the café, so mean and nasty now? I just could not understand.

Why is he staying in the room so long? Why? I hope he does not hurt Mama...he was so angry, I thought to myself. I wanted him to come out, to leave, so I could go back and be with my Mama. After what seemed like hours, he finally came out looking disheveled. His clothes were in disarray, and on his face he sported a big bloody scratch. He headed straight for the stairs, mounted them and left without even looking at me. I waited some time after the sound of his footsteps had completely faded away before I got up to go back into the room. I was afraid he would come back.

I quietly entered the room. Mama was lying on the bed, her back toward me, and her face turned toward the wall. The sound of very soft sobbing reached my ears. I climbed up on the bed, crawled under the covers and pressed my body against Mama's while placing my right arm over her back and shoulders. Almost in a whisper, I asked: "Mama, what's the matter? Why are you crying? Did that bad man hurt you? Don't be afraid, Mama, he is gone. I'm here. I'll take care of you."

The soft sobbing continued a little longer and then stopped. After I re-

FLORA M. SINGER   35

peated my question a few more times, instead of replying, she murmured: "Go to sleep my sweet Floreke, go to sleep my child."

I had no choice but to accept that because I knew when to press for explanations and when not to, and this was a time when I could not press.

I have never been able to forget that night. Many times, when I least expect it, this incident springs to my mind and haunts me, especially during nights when sleep eludes me.

CHAPTER 4

Surviving Antwerp

With smuggling no longer an option, Mama had to find another way to feed us and pay the rent. She managed to obtain an illegal job in a small neighborhood restaurant outside the main part of the city, where she cooked, served the clients, and sometimes functioned as cashier. The owner of the restaurant and Mama agreed that as part of the payment for Mama's work, we would be allowed to come to the restaurant in the early evening after closing time at five-thirty and eat the day's leftovers. This was great. We couldn't wait to get to the restaurant and have our supper. If we wasted no time we could eat and get home before curfew.

To supplement our income, Mama also took in a lodger, Mr. Juda Appel. Herr Appel, as we called him, was an immigrant who had arrived in Antwerp shortly before the invasion. Mama later learned from him that he had lost his wife and four children during a pogrom in his native Poland. Herr Appel was a dour man who never smiled, and my sisters and I did not like him.

Mama kept telling us to be nice to him and that he was sad because he missed his family. She did not, however, tell us why his family was not with him or what had happened to them. When we tried to approach him and talk to him, he always waved us away with the back of his hand. After a while we became tired of trying to be friendly and just left him alone.

During working hours, my sisters and I took care of the household. Even Betty, who was only five years old, had chores assigned to her. I was the supervisor, and for a while life seemed almost normal except for the constant struggle to get enough food to eat. Mama also began sewing again and managed to get it done in the few free hours she had left each day.

The shrill screams of air raid sirens continued to disrupt our days and nights. When they sounded, we ran into the cellar until the all clear. Also adding to the steady atmosphere of fear were the young fascists who began riots on our street and abused people, usually Jews. In addition, occasionally a van would pull up in our neighborhood and Gestapo men would jump out, enter a building and come out with two or three individuals, now under arrest, who were pushed into the back of the van. Then the van would take off. The Gestapo seemed to arrest only males, teenagers and adults. Sometimes the Gestapo men came once a week, sometimes twice. Sometimes they did not come for two weeks or more, but they always came.

One day Herr Appel decided to go out for a walk. He had not done this since he had moved into our spare room. I was surprised when I saw him putting on his jacket, carefully place his hat on his head, take his cane, and head for the door. Audaciously, I asked him, "Herr Appel, where are you going? Are you not taking a big risk?" He responded in a kinder tone than usual, "I am going out for a walk." What could I say? He was an adult and I was a child. My sisters were also surprised. They looked at me and we all shrugged our shoulders.

But Herr Appel never returned from his walk. He was arrested. Some time later he was somehow released and returned to Antwerp, but he never returned to the room in our apartment. He found other lodgings.

One day in April, a neighbor knocked on our door and, in an agitated voice, told us to quickly follow her to one of the principal synagogues in Antwerp. When we got there, there was a large crowd – Jews and non-Jews blocking our view. As we managed to edge closer to the synagogue, we watched in horror as Black Shirts, our name for the Belgian Fascists, threw Torah scrolls and prayer books out into the street and set fire to them and then to the synagogue.

Fire engines parked nearby stood idle as the synagogue burned. The firemen just stood around or lounged against the engines. I wondered why the firemen were not trying to extinguish the fire. I asked Mama and she silently shrugged her shoulders. She had no answer for me. A short time later, police began dispersing the crowd. Mama and I were suddenly gripped by fear as we made our way back home. We held hands tightly.

A few days later, when Mama was at work, a group of young fascists came into our street, broke windows and destroyed Jewish property. I learned later that this particular visit by the Black Shirts was prompted by a showing of the Nazi antisemitic film, *Der Ewige Jude* ("The Eternal Jew") at their meeting earlier that day.

Several of the young antisemites broke the display windows of the Jewish bookshop across the street from our building. Then they broke the glass of the shop's door, entered and pulled the owner of the shop, an elderly man, out into the street. While one Black Shirt pulled the old man by his beard, two others pulled his *peyot*, his sidecurls. They then threw him to the ground in the middle of the street, and kicked him with their boots as he lay there helpless, screaming in Yiddish to God, *"Raboyneh Sheloylem...helf mir!"* (Creator of the Universe, help me!). One of the fascists jumped on the old man's abdomen and danced on his prostrate body. Soon the old man fell silent. My sisters and I watched all of this helplessly from our apartment window, standing at the side of the window so as not to be seen from the street.

Charlotte was very upset and started to sob loudly. I slapped her face to quiet her because I was afraid someone would hear her and come to hurt us. She quieted down after that, and I hugged her to reassure her. Fortunately, no one heard her. Most likely no one could, yet we were terrified and easily panicked.

Betty stood by quietly, but her face reflected her fear. I pushed both my sisters away from the window, but I continued looking down. After the old man fell silent and no longer moved, the perpetrators rolled him to the side of gutter with their boots, then laughed as they left.

After a long interval several Jewish men came out of their homes, picked up the old Jew and took him inside. I was too afraid to let my sisters go to the restaurant to meet Mama, so we stayed in the apartment, hungry. When Mama came home, she already knew about what had happened to the old man from people who regularly ate at the restaurant. People were terribly frightened, and Mama complimented me on my decision not to come to the restaurant.

It seemed that the German occupier's goal was to make life as difficult as possible for the Jewish residents of Antwerp. Occasionally, Belgian policemen accompanied by the Gestapo would go to the Pelikaanstraat and into the surrounding streets, like ours, on their way to the Stadtpark. They stopped Jews at random and had them empty their pockets, ordering them to throw their wallets and other items onto the pavement. They then would proceed to transfer the valuables to their own pockets, laughing loudly the entire time. When they finished stuffing their pockets, they threw the empty wallets back onto the pavement. I witnessed one of these incidents while running an errand for Mama, frightening me greatly. But these thugs rarely hit a jackpot. The majority of the Jewish residents of Antwerp were not wealthy and belonged mostly to the hardworking middle class. Like my parents, many were refugees from Eastern Europe during the late 1920s or had arrived during the last peaceful years prior to the war.

The German authorities implemented a program of forced labor. The men called for duty were told that if they presented themselves voluntarily, their families would be safe from harm. As a good husband and father, Uncle Alex registered because he hoped by doing so it would help protect his family. And so he, his brother Adolph and other men in the family reported to the designated address. For their conscientiousness, they were sent as forced laborers to the Limbourg region coal mines. We would not see them again for three months.

A few months later they were called again and sent to northern France. I don't know what kind of work they did there, but I do know that when Uncles Alex and Adolph returned home they looked awful. They had lost a great deal of weight and their faces looked haggard and very tired. It seemed to me that they also looked much older. These once usually very talkative, smiling men were now very quiet and shared very little of their experiences with any of us.

When they were called up a third time. Mama felt that the men were being trapped in a game of cat and mouse and urged them not to respond. At first, Aunt Lea, Mama's youngest sister and Alex's wife, argued against Mama, because they felt it made more sense not to run afoul of the law. After a lengthy discussion they both agreed Mama's intuition and perceptions had been right in any number of situations, so they decided to agree with her. Uncle Alex then immediately left for Brussels to avoid the call-up and as soon as he found an apartment there risked returning to Antwerp to make arrangements to move the family. For a hefty fee a mover filled a truck with the contents of their apartment and moved them to Brussels. There, with their little boy, Nounou, they took an illegal apartment on the Place de la Cage aux Ours in Schaerbeek, a quiet neighborhood. We learned from a visitor that they were safely settled. Then Uncle Adolph and his wife, Estera, followed them there a short time later.

Meanwhile, with all this was happening around us, we children continued to play. I still visited Heleneke, who lived on the same street as we did. Her father, whom we called Uncle Muniek, was no longer home. He had been called up for forced labor and was also hiding in Brussels. Her mother, Rachel, and the children were prepared to follow him, but were waiting to receive word for a Brussels address.

Whenever Heleneke and I spent time together before the restrictions, we played hopscotch on the sidewalk. But now we no longer played outdoors, so we figured out how we could amuse ourselves. One game we played was dress shop, which I loved. Heleneke, who was the only girl in her family, had many beautiful dresses that her mother had made for her. She was always the sales lady and I was the client, and every time we played, I told the sales lady I was interested in looking at and trying on a light blue dress and cape ensemble. With Papa in America, Mama had no time to make us dresses, especially dresses with matching capes.

But Heleneke had exactly such a light blue dress ensemble in her wardrobe, an outfit that filled me with envy. My favorite part of the dress was the flared skirt, which fluttered up and outward whenever Heleneke twirled round and round, and when she wore the cape she looked just like a princess. I loved that beautiful dress and cape and knew that one day it would be mine because Heleneke's dresses and coats were handed down to me when she outgrew them. Although she was only six days older than me, she was much taller and grew faster.

When we played, I would put on the dress and twirl about in front of the mirror, watching the skirt flutter around me. I put the cape on over my shoulders with the help of "the sales lady" and glanced at my image in the mirror, feeling especially beautiful. After a while I would reluctantly take off the ensemble and put on my own clothes to go home, but the thought was always there: The ensemble would one day be mine. I was impatient and wished that Heleneke would grow a little faster.

I loved Heleneke. I was so glad that she and her family lived so close by, diagonally across the street from us. I was nostalgic for the Sundays before the difficult times when family members used to meet in the Antwerp Stadtpark to picnic and play. Heleneke, her older brother, Louis, (who was my first crush), Charlotte, and I would play together or watch the swans in the park's lake. Then, when Uncle Alex took out his mandolin and began to play, we would join the other family members in song. While we sang, I used to look at our group and feel lucky to be part of such a beautiful family. With the exception of Aunt Lea, Mama's sister, we were not related biologically, but no one thought about the details. We were family – uncles, aunts and "cousins."

Once Uncle Alex and his family moved away, things began to change rapidly. Uncle Alex's sister, Chany, her husband, Mendel, and their two sons, Jackie, who was almost fifteen years old, and Henry, three, also escaped. Soon Heleneke's family left as well, and then it was only the four of us, Mama, Charlotte, Betty and I, alone in Antwerp.

During the 1930s and the Depression, unemployment was rampant in many european countries. Individuals searching for jobs to feed their families often went to work in adjoining countries. Papa knew such an individual, Karl Frischbier, who came looking for and found work in Antwerp. Papa and Karl, who was a German, once worked together on a ship and became close friends. Usually, when Karl had a few days free, he would go to Germany to visit his family and friends. When work kept him in Antwerp, he would visit our family and sometimes spend the weekend at our apartment. My sisters and I loved Karl. It mattered little to any of us that Karl was a Christian and we were Jewish. He, in turn, was very respectful of our tradition when he occasionally spent Friday evenings with us and shared our Sabbath meal.

After Papa left for the United States, Karl still visited, but less often. Then his visits became rarer and rarer until one day after a visit, he kissed us good-bye. Mama said that she had a feeling we would perhaps never see Karl again.

One day early in 1942, Mama was rushing home on the Lange Kievitstraat, trying to get off the street before curfew. A man in uniform, a German uniform, called her name. She quickly glanced behind her, and when she saw a German officer, she became frightened. She thought she was going to be arrested and that we children would be left alone, a thought she could not bear. She started to run. The tall man in the uniform rapidly caught up with her, took her by the shoulders, turned her toward him, and said, "Fani, it's me, it's Karl. Don't be afraid…"

She recognized him and blurted out, "What in the world are you doing in that … uniform?" What audacity on Mama's part. She dared to ask a German what he was doing wearing his country's military uniform. Karl, not responding to her remark, asked how she was, how Papa was, and how the children were faring. She told Karl that Papa was safely in America, and that we were fine, but that everything was quite difficult for us, as he must know.

He asked if we had enough food. Mama told him Jews did not receive food ration stamps, so food was hard to find, that we never had enough to satisfy our hunger. She also told him, because she trusted him completely, that she had been working illegally in a restaurant, but had just lost her job because the owner did not have enough business.

At great risk, Karl began visiting us regularly; bringing us food every time he came. We were very lucky Karl had arrived just in time. I did not realize the danger he placed himself in by visiting us, and though we shared our food with our Jewish neighbors, some of them started to question Mama constantly – "What are you doing with that German?"

Mama told them about our prewar family friendship with Karl, but they could not accept it. They were afraid of him. Finally, Mama, with great difficulty, asked Karl to stop visiting. He understood, and did not come for a while. Then Karl started coming by after dark, in secret, to drop off a package of food and quickly leave. Eventually, the visits became more and more irregular. The time period between visits also grew longer until they stopped altogether. We missed him and we also missed the food he brought us.

In 1942, the situation for Jews in Antwerp went from bad to worse. Violent "incidents," as the police called them, by members of the Belgian fascist organizations, like the Vlag (the Flag), grew increasingly frequent. Not going to school and having to wear the yellow Star of David patch with the letter "J" in the center of our outer garments made life really miserable.

One day, my sisters and I decided to go for a walk to the Stadtpark at the end of our street. We did not know an order had been issued forbidding Jews to enter municipal parks. As we entered, a guard came to meet us, waving his finger to indicate that we were not allowed to enter. We were stunned. This was our park. This was the park we played in almost daily. I shrugged my shoulders, indicating my puzzlement to the guard who was a Belgian, not a German. But he continued walking toward us, silently waving his finger, forcing us to walk backwards out of the park. We returned home devastated.

Why? Why? What did we do to be forbidden to walk in the park where we had spent the years of our childhood? Why was being Jewish a crime?

One late evening, after dark, Karl arrived unexpectedly at our door. We had not seen him for several months. Mama was surprised and concerned.

Karl appeared agitated and nervous. He spoke rapidly and told my mother, "Fani, take the children and leave Antwerp immediately. Waste no time. Don't tell anybody; just go as quickly as you can."

Mama was shocked and did not immediately understand what Karl was saying – the words she understood, but not what he meant – and asked why. What was the reason for this sudden directive? He had come and had not even greeted us. His usual jovial warmth and the hugs we came to expect were not there. Just this order, to go … When Mama asked her question, he threw his arms up in the air, turned on his heels, and as he was leaving, said, "Just do as I say, ask no questions, and don't say anything to anyone."

Mama did as she was told. She removed the yellow stars from our garments and scraped the fabric with her fingernails so the outline of the star on the garment was erased and there were no signs of thread and needle holes. She then made each of us put on double layers of clothing because we were not going to take any suitcases that would alert anyone to our departure. Once we were dressed and ready to leave, Mama took the albums with the family photos and placed them in a tote bag. (In one of the albums there was a photograph of Heleneke wearing her light blue ensemble, the one I dearly wanted.) Then she gave us instructions on how to behave and act on the trip. We left just as the dawn gave way to the day.

Our instructions were to act as if we were on an outing to the capital. We walked down the Lang Kievistraat, then the Pelikaanstraat, to the Antwerp central train station. As we strolled along, we attempted to look as casual as possible. We talked about what we were going to see in Brussels, like the Manneke Pis (a small but very famous sculpture/fountain that recalled an act that saved the city of Brussels from destruction), and other sights. Once at the train station, Mama bought four tickets for Brussels because that was where everyone in the family had gone.

We took our seats in one of the train compartments and silently prayed we would arrive safely. We were far from being out of danger. True, we had removed our identifying yellow stars, but the identification card Mama carried was not green, like that of a Belgian citizen. Hers was yellow, with the dangerous red markings across it, indicating she was a foreigner and a Jew.

We knew we were safe as long as the train was not stopped. But during the war it was not unusual for trains to be stopped in the middle of a trip. The trains would be flagged and then the Gestapo would board and go through the cars asking people for their papers. Those not possessing the *right* documents were taken off the train for further investigation and possible arrest. We were fortunate as the train on this trip was not stopped. When we arrived in Brussels's Gare du Nord, all we had to worry about was exiting the station without encountering a checkpoint.

As we left the train, we noticed a crowd blocking the staircase that led from the train platforms to the exit. There was a checkpoint and people's official documents were being randomly checked. Mama quickly whispered to us, "Pick a fight." We immediately understood and obeyed, instinctively sensing what Mama meant and why. We sensed the lurking danger and reacted appropriately. We began to pull each other's hair and to push each other. People anxiously waiting in the queue to descend and get past the checkpoint became annoyed. In order to get rid of us, they moved aside and opened up a passage to let us through, which was exactly what Mama had hoped would happen as a result of our disturbance.

But we were not yet safely past the checkpoint, so we continued to quarrel as we descended the stairs. When we reached the bottom, the Germans manning the checkpoint stopped us. To our amazement, instead of asking Mama for her identity card, they told us to leave. One of the German officers, addressing Mama, said in German in a harsh voice: "Get those brats out of here." Mama understood what he said, and so did we, because we spoke Yiddish at home. But we pretended not to understand what he was saying to us – because he might immediately suspect that we were Jewish. So we did not move. We stood still and waited. Finally, after what seemed an eternity but was probably no more than a few minutes, one of them spoke to Mama in a broken, thick, accented French: *"Allez-vous en avec les gosses!"* ("Get out of here with those kids!") He didn't have to tell us twice. We left, not daring to move too quickly, though we really wanted to run as fast as we could.

Once we left the train station and put some distance between ourselves and the Germans, we looked at each other and took a deep breath. Then, with a sigh of relief, we continued to Uncle Alex and Aunt Lea's apartment on the Place de la Cage aux Ours. The Place, a town square, was actually a circle with a small park in the center. In the middle of the park stood a rock formation that contained a cave with bars at its entrance. Before the war, two bears actually lived in it. But they were gone when we arrived in Schaerbeek, Brussels, in the summer of 1942.

CHAPTER 5

Brussels

Uncle Alex and Aunt Lea were happy to see us. They had worried about us being left alone in Antwerp after everyone else had fled and told us they felt somewhat safe, that the Jewish people in Brussels were more dispersed – unlike Antwerp, where most Jewish residents lived in homogenous neighborhoods. They felt it was easier to blend in with the general population and were not as easily identifiable. They also introduced us to a kind neighbor, Mme. Petoud, whom they had taken into their confidence. She knew we were all Jewish and tried to help whenever and wherever she could.

Mama asked after the other family members in Brussels and Uncle Alex told her they were safely settled in different neighborhoods across the city. I thought about Heleneke and wondered, now that the weather was good again, if she had taken the light blue ensemble with her to Brussels.

A few days after our arrival in Schaerbeek, Mama, who was walking around with a troubled look on her face, told me that I needed to go back to Antwerp to warn the Jews in our old neighborhood. Warn them of what? She did not really know, but she remembered Karl's insistence that we leave immediately. At the time of his warning she did not dwell on his reasons. She had moved and acted like an automaton. Now, Mama wanted me to go back to Antwerp. Why me? Because, she said, "It's safer for a child than an adult; you won't be suspected. Just don't talk to any strangers. Deliver the message, then, without dawdling, come back immediately to Brussels."

My instructions were to leave on one of the earliest trains the following morning. After arriving in Antwerp I was to go the Lange Kievitstraat, warn some of our old neighbors, and tell them to warn everyone else. Warn them of what? What should I tell them? Mama told me to just say that something terrible was going to happen and that they would be wise to escape from the city. Since I was younger than fifteen, and did not as yet have to carry an official identity card, I could probably carry out this task and be back in Brussels by nightfall.

I bought my ticket at the Gare du Nord and took the train back to Antwerp. It was early in the morning, the station was quiet and the train was almost empty. I took a seat near a window and looked out during the forty-minute trip. I spoke to no one and the only contact I had with another person on the train was with the conductor, who collected my ticket. When I got to Antwerp, I left the Central Station and walked along the Pelikaanstraat to the Lange Kievitstraat. I turned left into the tunnel under the railroad tracks that led to our part of the street. When I exited from the tunnel into the open street, I encountered an eerie emptiness and quiet. I walked to the building where we had lived and rang a bell at random. No one answered. I rang another bell, then another, and another ... I reached no one. I tried the front door and it gave way. It was open. I went into the building. I knocked on apartment doors. No one answered. I climbed floor after floor, repeatedly knocking on doors, to no avail. I found it strange that no one was home on any floor. Finally, I left our building, crossed the street and entered the Leuwerikstraat.

The Leuwerikstraat is where the butcher shop, the grocery store and the bakery were located. But that street was also quiet. None of the shops were open. Some of the windows were boarded up because they had been broken during the last rampage by young Nazi sympathizers. Time was passing and I had not accomplished my task. I had not found anyone to warn. I was puzzled and started to be afraid. Where was everyone? I tried not to panic. I could not return to Brussels without warning a single person. Mama would be angry.

It was getting late with daylight turning to dusk. I had to return to Brussels. I decided to walk down one more street and entered the Somersstraat that straddled the Leuwerikstraat. As I walked along, pondering my next move, I heard some noise at the level of my ankles coming from a cellar window. I crouched down and looked at the window from which I thought the sounds came and saw a hand motioning me to come in. I entered the building and went down to the cellar. There I found a few people. I don't recall the exact number, perhaps six or eight.

I gave them Mama's message and I also told them how strange I thought it was that the streets and the neighborhood seemed so empty. I was not yet twelve years old and did not yet completely grasp the enormity of what was happening. I knew and I didn't know. I recognized every person in that cellar. They were friends and former neighbors. I gave them Mama's message. They told me that it was too late, that several trucks had pulled into the neighborhood's streets. The Gestapo had entered the neighborhood's buildings, chased people out, then loaded them into the trucks and took them away.

I told the people in the cellar that they should come with me. They responded that they had enough food stored in the cellar to last them for about two to three weeks, and they would stay there; that no one knew they were in that cellar.

I tried to insist that they come with me, but they refused. I left the cellar and, with leaden feet, walked back down the Leuwerikstraat and the Lange Kievitstraat toward the Pelikaanstraat and the train station. Night started to fall and I became frightened. When I saw someone in a uniform, I tried not to look at them and just continued on my way. I arrived at the Central Station, took the train and arrived in Brussels safely.

When Mama and I saw each other again we both took a deep breath, and when she hugged me, she held me tighter and longer than usual. I told her I had delivered the message to the people in the cellar on the Somersstraat and what I had learned from those hiding there. Mama was shocked when I told her that trucks had entered our neighborhood in Antwerp just after we had left and that the Gestapo had filled the trucks with Jews they had removed from their homes and arrested.

When Mama heard this, she finally understood the reason for Karl's urgent request that we leave Antwerp immediately. A terrible guilt began to gnaw at her for not telling anyone and for having respected his insistence that we not tell anyone. Of course, at that time she didn't know why we had to leave. There was no precedent for what had happened. Mama felt she *should* have suspected something and *should* have shared Karl's warning before we left, though she knew nothing. As a mother, her total focus was on getting her three children out of Antwerp per Karl's orders. She hadn't thought beyond that. There was no time. Now she suffered guilt, but there was nothing to do about it.

Uncle Alex, Aunt Lea and Nounou shared their small apartment with us for a while, but we were very crowded. Though the landlord, Mme. Petoud, did not allow that many people to live in a small single apartment, she gave us permission to stay in Uncle Alex and Aunt Lea's apartment until we could find a place of our own.

Mme. Petoud also introduced us to her friends, Monsieur and Mme. Fiers, an older couple who lived at 83 Rue François-Joseph Navez. A ten-minute walk from the Place de la Cage aux Ours, the building had an empty apartment available for rent on the second floor, directly across from the Fiers' apartment. The Fiers introduced us to their cousins, who owned the building, and also lent us their name. We became the family Fiers in August 1942.

The apartment consisted of three adequately sized rooms. There was a kitchen with a coal stove, suitable for cooking and heating, and a sink with running cold water. There was also enough space for a table and chairs. One room would serve as combination sitting room and bedroom for Mama and the other as a bedroom for Charlotte, Betty and me. There was a door at the back of the kitchen that led to a balcony that faced the solid brick wall of an adjoining building. To the right of the balcony, we could see railroad tracks, and trains rolled by regularly and noisily throughout the day and night.

The apartment had no bathing facilities. To bathe, we filled a cooking pot with water, heated it on the stove, then poured it into a bowl and washed ourselves. When we had no coal, we used cold water directly from the sink. Monsieur and Mme. Fiers showed us how to collect coal that fell from the trains onto the railroad tracks. Often, we got a good supply from trains transporting overloaded coal cars. We also learned when the trains ran and when not, so we could safely collect coal during the lull between the train runs.

Monsieur and Mme. Fiers also helped us get some second-hand furniture, bedding, linens, pots and pans, cooking and eating utensils and dishes. In addition to some basic staples, they also brought us fresh vegetables and fruit.

They never asked Mama for any ration stamps, knowing that we did not have any stamps or money. Mama kept telling them how grateful she was and offered them her engagement ring, the last piece of valuable jewelry she still had beside her wedding ring and wristwatch. They refused to take it and told her to keep it in case she needed it in the future. Mama reiterated how grateful she was for their help and promised that some day she would reimburse them for everything. They brushed her off by waving their hands and pursing their lips, as if what they were doing for us was merely a trifle. They smiled and placed their arms around her in a protective manner, the way parents would to reassure a child.

The summer months passed uneventfully for us, but all around us tragedy swirled. Through the Fiers and the Petouds we heard of the arrests and transports to the transit camp of Malines. We did not leave the apartment often and when we did, it was only to visit Uncle Alex, Aunt Lea and Nounou. Occasionally we spent a little time in the small park on the Place de la Cage aux Ours, but we were careful not to talk to anyone we didn't know. Through Aunt Lea, we met Martha, owner of a small bakery and pastry shop on a corner of the Place de la Cage aux Ours, directly across from the building they lived in.

When September rolled around and we were supposedly safely settled in Schaerbeek, Mama decided that we had to go back to school. It was a risky thing to do, but she enrolled us under our *nom de guerre*, Fiers, in the local public school on Rue Capronnier, a short walk from our apartment. We used our own secular first names, since they were neutral, and both Mama and Mme. Fiers came with us the day we were enrolled in the school, just in case there were questions.

Mama had given us strict instructions not to reveal to anyone that we were Jewish, or that the name we were using was a *nom de guerre*. The most difficult part of our assignment was not being able to tell Jewish students, who were wearing the yellow star, that we were Jews. While in Antwerp Jewish students could no longer attend public school, but the order had not as yet been implemented in Brussels and its surrounding suburbs.

Keeping this secret was very different from the childish games we used to play when we pretended to be other people. It is amazing that even Betty, who was not yet six years old, knew how important it was to keep our identity a secret.

Monsieur and Mme. Fiers were wonderful neighbors and friends, and helped Mama find illegal work, cleaning the home of the Hotton family who lived across the street from the school we attended. Mama was able to earn some vitally needed francs and was also given food by Madame Hotton.

Sometimes, Mama would stay at the Hotton home after she finished her regular day's work to serve and help clean up whenever the Hottons entertained guests. Whenever her work lasted beyond the evening curfew, she would stay at the Hotton home and spend the night in a small room in their attic. The Hottons were kind, caring people, but their son, to their great distress, eventually joined the Belgian Fascists and collaborated with the Nazis.

For the next few weeks life took on a routine that almost seemed normal. We went to school. We returned to our apartment. We did homework. When Mama did not get home in time, it was my job to prepare our meager supper while supervising my two sisters. If needed, I would help Charlotte and Betty with their homework. Then I would set the table for supper and started on my own homework while waiting for Mama to come home. If it was past curfew, I knew Mama would spend the night at the Hottons', but we would not eat until curfew, because we preferred to wait for her. After we ate, we cleared the table. Betty reluctantly wiped the table clean. Charlotte washed the dishes carefully, taking care not to splash any dirty water on her clothes. I dried the dishes, swept the floor, pulled down the blackout window shades and returned to my homework.

It was difficult to do homework once darkness fell because the lighting in the apartment was very dim. When the three of us were sleepy we would curl up together in Mama's bed, because when she wasn't home we were afraid, and sleeping together somewhat alleviated our fear. This was especially true when the air raid sirens sounded. But now we never went into the bomb shelters. Mama said the fewer people we had contact with, the better.

On weekends and school holidays we were free to visit Aunt Lea's family. Occasionally we would venture out of the immediate neighborhood on walks with Aunt Lea and Uncle Alex to visit other family members. As taught by Mama, we never dawdled or made any eye contact with anyone we passed.

Then, after several weeks at school, I was called into the principal's office and was asked to tell Mama that the principal wished to speak with her and that she must come to the school. I protested, because Mama had to work, and asked her why Mama had to come to school, for in my child's mind, the only time a principal wanted to see a parent was because the child needed to be punished. I didn't understand what I had done wrong.

"Why does my mother have to come to school; why do you wish to speak with her? We are behaving ourselves. We have been good. I have been good; my sisters have been good. Please don't ask my mother to come to school." Seeing my distress, the principal quickly reassured me that, indeed, we had been behaving ourselves, but she wished to speak to our mother about another matter. I delivered the message to Mama with trepidation, hoping she would believe me when I told her that the principal's request had nothing to do with our behavior at school.

Still, I kept wondering why she wished to speak with Mama. Perhaps it was related to our schoolwork, because we were having some difficulty with the language. In Antwerp children were taught in Flemish, the primary language of the region and French was taught as a second language in the fifth grade. In Brussels, classes were held in French, and to the best of my recollection, Flemish was neither taught nor spoken.

So Mama went to school to see and speak with the principal. It seemed that the principal suspected that we were Jewish children when we enrolled and, therefore, had not asked Mama for documents verifying our legal status, as required by law. When she confronted Mama with her questions, Mama vehemently denied that we were Jewish. The principal reassured her that she could be trusted, that she had our well-being at heart and only wished to help us.

We had to learn to trust people when they offered help, because it was very difficult to survive without the help of others. Even when help was offered freely, there were risks involved in accepting it. However, we had little choice if we wanted to live. The principal told Mama that it was too dangerous for the three of us to remain at the school. She told Mama about an incident Mama was familiar with because I had told it to her.

Just the day before, two German officials came to the school and visited several classrooms, one of which was mine. It turned out that the principal and teaching staff were terrified of one particular third-grader, a girl whose older brother was a member of the Brown Shirts, the Belgian Nazis. Whenever this student was reprimanded by a teacher or disagreed with a classmate, she threatened to "tell" her brother. The situation was therefore extremely dangerous and the principal offered to introduce Mama to a gentleman who, she said, might be able to help us, for she felt it was time for us to go totally "underground." This was what led to a meeting in the principal's office several days later, where Mama was formally introduced to a man named George Ranson.

Who was Monsieur Ranson? Ranson was a patron of the public school on Rue Capronnier. He was a member of a local group of residents in Schaerbeek who provided the school with classroom and library supplies they could not get from the district's Department of Education. The group also helped needy students and donated items like milk and winter coats – whatever was needed. My sisters and I were beneficiaries of this largesse. That fall, we each were served a glass of milk daily and we were given woolen coats to keep us warm during the coming winter months.

Monsieur Ranson was an industrialist, the proprietor of a local factory that manufactured technical equipment. Like all factories in occupied Belgium, his factory fell under the control of the Nazis and all production was directed to benefit the German war machine. Secretly, Monsieur Ranson was also a member of the Belgian Resistance. During the day all work in the factory was directed to benefit the Germans, but in the evenings other items were secretly produced in the cellar. These items were made by and for the members of the Resistance, to help Belgium's cause. Several of these Resistance members were regular employees in the Ranson factory.

A few days after Mama met Monsieur Ranson, the principal again asked me to summon Mama to her office. She told me that she had important news for Mama. This time I accompanied Mama to the principal's office. Monsieur Ranson was already there waiting for us. He stood up to greet us as the principal asked us to sit. Then the principal turned to Mama and explained why Monsieur Ranson had wanted to meet with her. He wanted to help. I listened quietly, frightened.

Monsieur Ranson told Mama that the situation for Jews was deteriorating and that the Nazis were accelerating their arrests. It was suggested that we girls stop coming to school. He gave us a forged identity card showing our family name as *Fiers* and gave Mama a gold necklace bearing a Christian cross pendant, suggesting she wear it at all times. The necklace belonged to his wife, who graciously allowed him to lend it to Mama. Monsieur Ranson also offered Mama employment as an Aryan, a non-Jew, in his factory. We needed the income badly, so this was good news, because food on the black market was outrageously expensive.

After the meeting we stayed away from school and confined ourselves to the apartment on Rue François-Joseph Navez. During school hours, we had to be totally silent and not walk around on squeaky floors, even in our socks, lest someone suspect there were children in the apartment while school was in session. We could not even turn on the faucet to get a drink of water and prepared beforehand by filling a container like a pot or a bottle before Mama left for work. We were also forbidden to flush the toilet until evening. Then we were able to use the toilet because the kitchen door was very close to the toilet, which was on the balcony. We could slip in without being heard or seen, especially when a noisy train passed by.

During those hours we could not go near any of the windows, just in case a passerby would see us. As a result of all our restrictions, we spent our days reading books, drawing pictures and just lying on our beds until Mama would come home and we could move around normally. The days were long and boring, but more than that, every time I heard footsteps in the hall outside our door, I was afraid it might be the Gestapo.

CHAPTER 6

Fear

I lived in a constant state of tension, filled with fear for myself and for my sisters. The weekends were fairly normal, especially when Mama was home. For a while, it seemed we were living a normal life and were not hiding from anyone. We were comfortable with our assumed identity and visited our family where Monsieur and Mme. Petoud would join us on occasion and spend a few pleasant hours. Sometimes we took walks in the neighborhood, stopping at Martha's Boulangerie and Patisserie. Whenever we came in, Martha offered us children a treat. She sometimes gave Aunt Lea and Mama a loaf of bread or two without asking for either food ration stamps or money. Did she know we were Jewish at that time? I don't know.

One day, after visiting us in our apartment, Uncle Alex, Aunt Lea and Nounou were passing Martha's patisserie on their way home and noticed Martha standing in front of the shop as if waiting for someone. As soon as they were within earshot, Martha, without moving, without changing the neutral expression on her face, told them to turn back.

"Alex, Lea, turn around quickly; go back where you came from. They just raided your building…" My aunt and uncle understood immediately who *they* were, came back to our apartment and never left it again.

Madame Petoud had a key to the apartment and, a day later, brought them a few pieces of clothing and Uncle Alex's pattern cutting knife, the one he used to cut garments. He thought he might need it, just in case. They also saved cherished possessions like photo albums. The Petouds kept small items, including Uncle Alex's mandolin – the beautiful instrument that produced such wonderful music under his fingers – in their apartment for safekeeping. Under their own name, they placed large items, like furniture and household goods, into storage, including a Murphy bed that looked like a bookcase and came down to open as a double bed. When Mama realized that our own photo albums were at risk, she asked the Petouds to take them and keep them for us until the war was over. She completely forgot that she had slipped a yellow star into the album.

There were now seven people living in our small apartment, so Mama gave the family their own bedroom. We rearranged the sitting room to make ourselves as comfortable as possible. Charlotte and Betty, because they were the smallest, slept together on the couch. Mama and I slept on the floor. We all shared the kitchen and the single toilet. At this point no one dared use the toilet during the day. Although we were almost sure that no one could see us when we slipped into the toilet, we felt it was better to be cautious. Thus, during the day we used chamber pots that we emptied in the toilet after dark. To cover any noise, we only flushed when we heard flushing sounds from other toilets or when a train was passing.

From the day we were warned, Mama was the only person to leave the apartment. She left every morning at dawn to go to work in Ranson's factory and returned just before the evening curfew. She would often bring home a package of food provided by Monsieur Ranson. The Fiers would also bring us food. But even with the help of these kind people, there was never enough to eat. Still, we learned to survive on what we received and were grateful. Through it all Charlotte never complained of hunger. She was quiet and sat sucking her thumb. Little Betty was hungry all the time and complained constantly. She could not understand why we didn't give her enough food. Being but six years old, how could she possibly understand our situation as Jews? I had difficulty understanding it myself. Everyone suffered. I knew that, but I couldn't understand why it was worse for Jews. What did we ever do to deserve this?

One late night, long after curfew, there was a knock on the door. Mama hesitated, because the knock was not the agreed upon code for people we knew. Who could it be? The Gestapo? Finally, after another knock, Mama opened the door and saw before her a bedraggled man, his face pale and drawn, his clothes soiled, with bloodstains on his shirt. Mama and I recognized him immediately. It was the same Polish man, Herr Juda Appel, who had lodged with us in Antwerp. He remembered Place de la Cage aux Ours and somehow managed to get our address from Mme. Petoud. We were surprised she had given it to him.

Mama gave him some water and a piece of buttered bread. While he devoured the bread, Mama and Aunt Lea cleaned some of the blood from the wounds that stained his shirt. He was very weak. After he ate, we placed some bedding on the floor of the sitting room to enable him to rest. He fell asleep almost immediately, and stayed asleep for several hours.

When he awoke, Mama, Uncle Alex and Aunt Lea gave him something to drink and asked him what had happened to him and the people in Antwerp after our departure for Brussels. We all sat around him on the floor and were anxious to hear what he had to tell us. There had been a raid and the Jewish residents of the Lange Kievitstraat and the surrounding neighborhoods were all taken away to a transit camp in the former army barracks of Mechelen. After being kept at the transit camp for a few days, under deplorable conditions, the people were loaded into trains consisting of empty boxcars. The people, he said, were packed in tightly, with hardly any space to even sit down on the floor.

Somehow, Herr Appel and a couple of other men were able to pry up some floor planks and squeeze themselves through to the tracks below. This was risky. The slightest mistake when they squeezed through would land them under the train wheels. Appel was lucky. He landed in the center of the train track and lay totally still until the train passed over him and was completely out of sight. Then he managed to get off the tracks and hide under some bushes until night fell. After dark, he made his way on foot to Brussels, not Antwerp. This journey, which would have taken less than an hour by train, took several days. When he squeezed through the ripped up floor boards and fell onto the track he was badly bruised and sustained several cuts that became infected. By the time he got to us, he was feverish and weak.

Juda Appel stayed with us for a few days. Aunt Lea and Mama tended to his wounds, but the infected wounds did not respond to their care. After a few days, Herr Appel weakly called Mama to his beside and said, "Fani, I'm afraid that my presence in the apartment could endanger all of you. Is there a way to find me another shelter, another place where I could be safe?" He insisted on leaving the apartment.

Mama and I found him a safe place in the ruins of a bombed-out building within walking distance. He stayed there while Mama and I returned to the apartment to fetch blankets and a pillow. Mama also wrapped up some food and filled a bottle with water, then sent me back with these items to his "new lodgings." For the next five or six days I regularly brought him some food, and every time I visited him he looked worse. The infection was spreading and we had no remedy for it. Mama asked George Ranson for help. The next time I brought him food, Mama told me to tell him that he would shortly receive help from a friend. As I made my way through the labyrinth of the building's ruins to his spot, I imagined how happy he would be when he heard the good news – that he would soon receive help and medical care.

But when I reached his hiding place, it was empty. No Juda Appel. Where could he be? I couldn't leave without telling him…he would be so happy to hear the good news. I searched through the ruins, thinking he might have found another, more comfortable spot. Finally, I gave up and returned to the apartment with the sad news that Juda Appel had disappeared.

We never saw Juda Appel again. The Nazi raids on Jews became more frequent now, even in Brussels. Monsieur Ranson told Mama that it would be safer for us, the children, if we were hidden in some place other than the apartment, a place separate from our family members. He offered to make arrangements for us. I was placed with Monsieur Ranson's family. Charlotte was sheltered in the home of George Ranson's brother, Henry, and Betty was placed in the home of George Ranson's secretary. He also offered to find a shelter for Nounou. Aunt Lea refused to be separated from her child, so he remained with his parents at our apartment on the Rue François-Joseph Navez.

George Ranson's family consisted of his wife, his daughter, Georgette, and two sons, Henry and Marcel. His daughter and I were about the same age, twelve. Mme. Ranson and her children treated me nicely, but did not spend much time with me. The children left early in the morning for school and Monsieur Ranson also left early to go to work.

During the day, Madame Ranson and I stayed home. While she attended to household duties, I kept myself quietly busy, reading books from the well-stocked bookcases I found throughout their home. I asked whether I could help with the household chores, but was turned down. Sometimes Madame Ranson left to shop for groceries, to go to the butcher shop, the bakery, or to run other errands. She was often gone for several hours because lengthy queues were normal everywhere during that time. I was lonely being by my-self in their home. But I was also fortunate because I loved to read and there were plenty of books from which to choose.

Whenever Madame Ranson returned home, she usually offered me something to eat. When she'd ask if I was still hungry and wanted more, I al-ways said no because of Mama's diligent training. I was taught never to admit that I was hungry and always to refuse a second helping. When the Ranson children returned home from school they nodded their heads in my direction, barely acknowledging my presence in their home. Then they had their after school snacks and settled down to do their homework. I was jealous. I wanted to go to school and have assignments, too, but I couldn't. I was Jewish.

I knew the Ranson children were not happy to have me in their home. Before I moved in they would often invite school friends to visit after school before settling down to do homework. With me in the house, they could no longer do this.

About two weeks after my arrival, we were eating supper around the kitchen table. Conversation was flowing between the children and their par-ents. They were talking about school, friends, and activities they participated in on that particular day. I was quiet. What could I say that would interest this family? I was not of their world. I did not share any of the children's activities. I did not attend school. I had no friends of my age in Brussels. I was being hidden in this home to protect me from the Nazi scourge. I should be grateful, if not happy.

When the meal was finished, I offered to help Madame Ranson wash the supper dishes. Afterwards I retired to the room assigned to me, undressed, put on my pajamas, and climbed into the bed. Monsieur Ranson knocked on the door, then came into the room and asked me if I needed anything. I politely said no and thanked him for asking. He wished me a good night, tucked my blanket in around me, gave me a kiss on the forehead, and walked out closing the door behind him.

The house was quiet and I felt myself drifting into sleep, when suddenly I heard Madame Ranson's voice. She spoke softly at first, but her voice rose gradually as she addressed her husband, "George, you want to work with the underground, you want to defy the law … you want to risk your life for a few Jews, that's fine … you have that right … but you don't have the right to risk my life and the lives of our children …"

I jumped out of bed and ran into the kitchen where the couple was arguing. I pulled on Monsieur's hand while I begged him, "Please Monsieur Ranson, please take me back to my mother. I don't want you and Madame Ranson to fight because of me, please."

He stopped speaking to his wife, turned to me, pointed his hand with outstretched forefinger at me, and in a harsh voice I had never heard him use before, he almost shouted at me: "You, get back into bed – immediately! This is none of your business!"

I became frightened. I had never seen this usually gentle person in such a state. I reacted immediately. I spun around and made a mad dash back into my room and jumped into bed, pulling the bed covers over my head. I didn't dare move for the rest of the night. Eventually I fell into a deep, dreamless sleep until I was gently awakened by Monsieur Ranson.

"It is time to get up, little one, we must talk."

He left the room. I got out of bed, filled the wash bowl with water from the pitcher that stood on the small table against the wall, washed and dressed, then joined Monsieur Ranson in the kitchen. The children and Madame Ranson had already left the house.

When I came into the kitchen, I noticed that Monsieur Ranson, who was waiting for me at the table, was again the kind gentle person I knew him to be. He had prepared breakfast for me. On the table, neatly placed, was a plate holding a slice of dark Belgian bread, which he had already buttered, and a glass of chocolate milk. What a luxury. I thanked him and started to eat while anticipating some dreadful news because of the seriousness of his usually smiling face. He let me eat and sat silently until I finished my slice of buttered bread. Then he approached the dreaded subject while I drank the chocolate milk. Although I did not know precisely what the content of our conversation would be I had a premonition, hoping against hope that I would be wrong.

He started slowly, hesitantly. "Little one, we have a problem. You can no longer stay in this house with us. It is too risky. But I have found a wonderful place for you and your sisters in the countryside, near the river, in the village of Doel. The place is a convent of the Sisters of Saint Francis. My cousin, Sister Odonia, lives in that convent and she has offered to hide you and your sisters there."

"What is so wonderful is that you will be together with your sisters and all three of you will be safe with my cousin." He continued, "We will probably leave in two days, as soon as I can make all the arrangements for transportation. I will personally take you there."

"Does Mama know?" I asked. He replied affirmatively and told me that my sisters and I would have the opportunity to see Mama before we left for the village. This pleased me immensely since I had not seen Mama for almost two and a half weeks and I missed her very much. I was also pleased that I would soon be with my two sisters again.

Before he left the apartment for work, he turned around and told me not to tell his children I would be leaving. He would tell them, explain, and say good-bye to them for me. He reminded me that when everyone else was out of the apartment not to answer the doorbell or any knock on the door, because no one was supposed to know that there was anybody in the apartment.

After he left, I retreated to "my" room to occupy myself with the only activity I freely engaged in without making any noise – reading. I immersed myself in the tales of Hans Christian Anderson, my favorites at the time. This distracted me and took me away from reality and my present fears.

On that same Wednesday evening in October, when Monsieur Ranson wished me goodnight, he quietly told me everything was arranged and that we would be leaving in two days – on a Friday morning. We would fetch my two sisters, see Mama for a short visit, and then leave for the convent in Doel.

That night sleep eluded me. I tried hard to fall asleep because it would stop me from being tortured by frightening thoughts. A convent? What was that precisely? I had a vague image of a dark place where ladies lived, ladies who wore dark somber clothing that covered their bodies and their heads completely, barely showing their faces and their hands.

Friday morning, while it was still dark and a streak of pale light had barely pierced the dark horizon to signal a new day, I asked Monsieur Ranson if he would allow me to take a book belonging to the family's library with me as I was in the middle of reading it. I promised to return it when I finished. He told me to ask Madame Ranson. I did and she said yes, and told me to keep the book as a gift. I thanked her for the book and her hospitality and asked her to greet the children for me when they got up. Then I followed Monsieur Ranson quietly out the door, down the stairs, and out to the deserted street. Monsieur Ranson climbed onto his bicycle and I climbed on behind him, sitting on the back rack and holding on to his waist as we rode to the factory without speaking.

When I went into Monsieur Ranson's office, I found Mama, Charlotte and Betty along with his brother Henri and his secretary. When I saw Mama's beautiful face and my two sisters, a wave of happiness washed over me. It is impossible to describe the joy I experienced when I saw them. Mama walked toward me with outstretched arms and tears in her eyes. The little ones were clinging to her. I joined them, competing for the space closest to her body. She hugged us tightly and kissed us on our cheeks, on our foreheads, wherever she could. When I kissed her back I was able to taste the salty tears running down her cheeks.

Monsieur Ranson explained that he was going to drive the open flatbed truck we would be taking out into the country. Each of us would be placed under an upside down empty wooden crate. Over and around these crates he would place crates filled with vegetables and fruits. He would be making occasional stops in safe, out-of-the-way places to give us something to eat and drink and to give us an opportunity to relieve ourselves behind a tree or bush. These stops, he explained, would also allow us to stretch our legs a bit, to relax them from the imposed immobility of sitting under the crates.

He strongly impressed upon us that unless he stopped and removed the crates from over us, we were not to move. This was something we would not be able to do anyway because the space under each crate was just barely enough for us, especially me, the tallest of the three. He said we were to be totally silent at all times, not to make a sound no matter what, unless he, Monsieur Ranson, gave us permission to speak.

My sisters and I held on to Mama. We did not want to release her from our embrace. I knew, and she knew, that my sisters and I would be leaving shortly, but whether we would see each other again was a question that could not be answered. All we could do is hope for an eventual reunion. Then Monsieur Ranson signaled that it was time to leave.

Mama then took me aside and told me "…Flora, you're the oldest. You're in charge of your sisters. Make sure they don't betray themselves. Make sure that they remember their *nom de guerre* at all times. Make sure that they remember their Jewish heritage. If the Gestapo catches me and I don't come back, go to Madame Petoud, she has the family photographs. Then find your father in America and take the girls to him." She stopped for a moment, and shaking her finger at me, said, "God help you, Flora, if something happens to you and your sisters." Finally, with great difficulty, we walked away from Mama to follow Monsieur Ranson to the small flatbed truck that stood waiting for us.

On the floor of the flatbed were the wooden crates Monsieur Ranson had talked about. With his help and that of his brother we climbed the platform of the truck. Before each of us was placed and hidden under our individual crates, we waved good-bye once more to Mama and threw her one last kiss.

When we were settled under the crates, Monsieur Ranson told us again that we would have to be totally quiet whenever the truck stopped unless he told us otherwise. He and his brother then covered and surrounded our crates with others filled with vegetables and fruits.

Traveling at this time was dangerous. The Germans had checkpoints everywhere, and vehicles were often stopped in order to check the vehicle registration and the driver's identity papers. Many times, the contents were also checked and examined if there was the slightest doubt of the driver's description of the contents. We were just at the outskirts of Brussels when the truck was stopped at such a checkpoint. I heard questions addressed to Monsieur Ranson in thick German accents. "Papers."

We heard them talking while apparently examining Monsieur Ranson's documents. There was no concern there. He was a Belgian citizen. He was a Christian. His identity card clearly reflected his status. "What are you carrying in your containers?"

"You can see for yourself. I am a merchant and I am making a delivery of fruits and vegetables."

They looked at his identity card. "Your card states your profession as an industrialist."

"But, monsieur," Georges Ranson replied, "it is wartime. One does what one can to feed one's family."

During this interrogation I sat under my crate like a tightly wound-up clock and imagined that my sisters, under their crates, were probably as tense as I was. I wanted to console them, to comfort them, especially little Betty, but I couldn't. I was dealing with a problem of my own. While the Germans were examining Monsieur Ranson's documents, I had a tickling and choking sensation in my throat. I knew that the only way to get relief from this was to cough, but of course I couldn't. If I coughed, the sound would alarm the men in uniform and that would lead to an examination of the crates' concealed contents. Then, when they found us, it would lead to our arrest as well as the arrest of Georges Ranson.

I also felt that if I didn't cough soon, I would choke to death. I decided then to choke to death in order to save the others from arrest. This was a very difficult decision for a twelve-year-old to make, but I felt that I had no other choice because if we were arrested, I would be killed anyway. This way only one of us would die, instead of all of us. This ticklish sensation in my throat had been with me since I was a little girl and several times it came close to giving me away when we were hiding. Part of my decision was also based on fear that, if something were to happen to my sisters, how could I ever explain it to my mother when we were reunited?

Apparently the men at the checkpoint found Monsieur Ranson's documents in order and were satisfied with his explanation regarding the contents of the crates. After a perfunctory examination of the top crates and banging on the sides of the filled vegetable and fruit crates, they allowed him to leave. When I heard the reassuring sounds of the truck motor's roar and rolling wheels on the pavement, I relaxed. When the truck had placed some distance between the checkpoint and us I allowed myself the delightful relief of a cough to clear my throat.

Once we reached the open countryside and were a good distance away from Brussels, Monsieur Ranson parked the truck on a quiet road near a grove of trees. He removed some of the upper layer of crates and allowed us to come out for a little while. The sensation of being able to stretch our legs was wonderful. I had never before really appreciated being able to stretch and move my body freely. We relieved ourselves behind the trees in the grove while Monsieur Ranson watched the area to make sure we were safe. When we came out we were treated to, what seemed to me, the most delicious buttered bread and pieces of apple. We did not dawdle either. As soon as we finished eating, we climbed back on the truck and were placed under the crates to continue our journey.

CHAPTER 7

The Convent

When we arrived at our destination it was late afternoon. Monsieur Ranson pulled up behind some buildings and helped us out of our hiding places. At the end of the street there stood a large church. The convent, attached to the church, was located on Doel's narrow main street. As we walked to the convent entrance, we clung to Monsieur Ranson, the little ones holding his hands and me holding on to one of the sleeves of his jacket. We were scared. We did not know what to expect in this strange place. We had never been inside a convent. Monsieur Ranson pushed the doorbell and we heard it ring with a hollow sound inside the building. A figure, dressed all in black except for a white collar and a white starched strip of fabric covering her forehead under a dark veil, opened the heavy door. We had never been this close to a nun. We occasionally saw one from afar, but this figure, all in black, was intimidating. Monsieur Ranson assured us she was kind.

Crossing a spacious, but somewhat dark foyer, we were shown into a parlor, a dark wood-paneled room in the middle of which stood a long rectangular table covered with a heavy cloth. Several chairs stood against a wall. The nun placed three chairs on one side of the table for the three of us, one on the opposite side of the table, and one at the end of the table, which I assumed was for Monsieur Ranson. The nun then left the room to fetch Monsieur Ranson's cousin, Sister Odonia. The same nun returned alone a short time later and apologized profusely to Monsieur Ranson because she had been unable to locate Sister Odonia at that moment. Georges Ranson could not wait. He had to return to Brussels, to get home before curfew.

He told the nun that the fruit and vegetables he had brought with him he wished to leave as a gift and asked her to find someone to help him unload the truck, which she went to do. He waited a few minutes and then said he would go and check to see what was happening and if there was someone to unload the truck. We wanted to go with him, to get our few belongings from the truck, but he told us to stay in the parlor, that he would make sure our things were brought to us. Before he left, he told us that he would tell Mama how well we behaved on the journey and gave us his word that the nuns were very nice and would treat us well; that we would be safe here. He warned us again to be careful, to be obedient and good. He hugged us good-bye, gave each of us a kiss on the forehead, and then left. I wanted to run after him; I felt we were abandoned, but I knew we had to stay. I was faced with a difficult task. I had to console my sisters, who wanted to go back to Mama. I did too, but...

The nun came back and sat with us silently, waiting. Charlotte, Betty and I sat and looked around the strange room. On the wall facing us hung a crucifix with a figure of Jesus on it. Suddenly, Betty, my youngest sister, asked the nun, "What is that?" pointing to the crucifix. "You know, little one, that is our Lord on the cross." I kicked Betty under to table to stop her from talking. She kicked me back and continued. She enjoyed the attention she was receiving from the nun. "I'm sure you have such a crucifix at home," continued the nun.

"No, we don't," Betty replied. "You don't?" What do you mean, you don't? What do you have then?"

As Betty was preparing to reply again, I pinched her thigh under the table – I was desperate. Charlotte's face reflected my fear, but neither of us could do anything, lest the nun suspect something. I did not know whether this particular nun was aware of the reason for our coming to stay in her convent. Betty was only six years old and did not as yet completely understand our delicate situation, the danger we were in, if we were discovered to be Jews.

She continued after pushing me with her elbow and telling me in a loud "whisper" to leave her alone. She continued talking to the nun. "I don't know what it is called, but if you give me a pencil and a piece of paper, I'll show you." The nun complied and Betty drew a beautiful, almost perfect Star of

David. I fell into a state of panic. All I could think of was that this was it. We were lost. The nun looked at the paper and her eyes opened wide. Charlotte and I thought they looked as they would pop out of her head. She made a dash for the door and disappeared.

I strongly reprimanded Betty, who started to cry, not knowing that what she did was so wrong. She thought she was being good when she replied politely to the nun's questions. I was overcome with guilt. I was the oldest and should be kinder to my little sister. By now, Charlotte had also started to cry, and I felt tears welling up in my eyes as well. Do not cry Flora, I thought, remember Mama's instructions to be strong, to take care of the two younger ones. I placed my arms around my two sisters, keeping them close to me. And thus we waited, silently. Suddenly, we heard several loud voices coming from the other side of the closed door.

The door opened and three nuns entered, talking in agitated voices, gesturing. Then, simultaneously they stopped and looked at the three of us. We recognized the nun who had been with us in the parlor earlier and was now joined by the other nuns. We soon learned she was the Mother Superior; the second one, the one with the gentle face and kind looking eyes, we learned, was Sister Odonia, Georges Ranson's cousin, and the third one, the small slight nun, the one with the mischievous look in her eyes, was Sister Odonia's best friend, Sister Roberta.

We learned much later that the confusion we were witnessing was caused by Sister Odonia. After having agreed to her cousin's request to shelter us, Sister Odonia never told her Mother Superior that the children who were coming to stay were Jewish. What she did say was that there were three children who needed a temporary home. Their mother was alone and fallen seriously ill and thus was not able to care for them until she recuperated. The children's father was a prisoner of war, interned in Germany. Sister Odonia had agreed to shelter the children as a special favor for her cousin, who had always been very generous toward her as well as to the other nuns of the convent.

Whenever the nuns had a need they knew they could turn to Georges Ranson. Now he needed a favor. The children, if caught, faced death. After a lengthy discussion of the implications and the risks of sheltering Jewish children, the Mother Superior allowed us to stay. All the nuns agreed with this decision. Sister Odonia came over to us and welcomed us with a big smile and a hug for each of us. We were the only children in the convent, since the parochial school, administered by these nuns of the Order of Saint Francis, had been closed since the beginning of the war.

We were given a room on the second floor that had a double bed and a cot for a single person, plus a desk and a big double door armoire for the few pieces of clothing we brought with us. Charlotte and Betty were told to share the double bed. I was assigned the cot. The first thing Betty noticed, again, was the crucifix on the wall above the bed. This time she said nothing, but as soon as the nun who had accompanied us to the room had left, she turned to me and pointing to the crucifix, said, "There is another one."

Sister Odonia, who had come up to assure herself that we were comfortable, suggested we rest for a while. We were exhausted from the journey, from the cramped spaces under the crates, from the fear of being discovered, and from being in this unfamiliar place without Mama. We were also filled with apprehension after meeting all these new people, the nuns, and not knowing what the next day would bring.

About a half hour after we were settled in our room, Sister Roberta brought up our belongings. They consisted of some clothing, toothbrushes, toothpaste, the book I was allowed to borrow from the Ranson's home and Betty's ragtag bear. Charlotte clutched an old little blanket she had brought with her. After we had put everything in its proper place, Sister Roberta asked us to follow her down to eat supper with the nuns. We were hungry and ate quietly, observing the nuns who were eating with us. After supper we were returned to our room for the night.

We adjusted quickly to life in the convent because of the kindness shown us by the nuns, especially Sister Odonia and her friend, Sister Roberta. We were given wooden clogs to wear instead of leather shoes. The clogs were not worn indoors; they were removed and left in the entrance vestibule when we came in from outdoors. To wear clogs properly you also had to wear crocheted woolen slippers as well as socks. Sister Roberta crocheted a pair of these woolen slippers for each of us and we loved them.

We did not attend school, but kept ourselves busy inside by reading, drawing and talking with the nuns. Here, in Doel, we were in the Flemish speaking part of Belgium and could speak our native Flemish as we had done in Antwerp. Sometimes we were allowed into the convent's library to look at the books. Many of them were biographies of people who became saints.

As we adjusted to the routine of life in the convent, we began to lose some of our fear. We learned the Catholic prayers we had to recite each morning on our knees at the side of our beds, as well as the prayers before eating and other activities. At home we had also recited prayers before eating and before going to bed, but they were Jewish prayers in Hebrew. Now we could no longer say them.

Sister Odonia and Sister Roberta took us on walks along the riverbank, where we enjoyed looking at the water and the occasional fishing boats; we loved talking with these two sisters, and at times I forgot why we were in Doel because it was so peaceful. We rarely saw any German soldiers and, when we did, they were usually far away from us. Sister Odonia told me that there was only a small contingent of German military personnel in Doel.

Before the war, there was a chaplain assigned exclusively to the convent. This chaplain's responsibilities consisted of conducting Mass in the chapel and rendering other religious services to the nuns. He listened to the nuns' confessions, officiated at the ceremony where the nuns took their vows, and conducted funeral services if a nun died. He also acted as the nuns' general counselor. But with the advent of the war, like all other Belgian males, the chaplain had been drafted into the army and was now a prisoner of war in Germany like many others. The nuns now attended Mass at the village church. The village priest would also come to the convent to hear confessions and to officiate when needed.

We always accompanied the nuns to the church for Mass on Sundays. When people greeted us, we smiled at them but kept quiet. Sister Odonia taught us, before our first excursion to the church, how to walk down the aisle with them, genuflect and then slide into the pew after them and sit down. We imitated all their actions. We stood up when they stood up, we kneeled when they kneeled, and sat down when they sat down. As learned, we crossed ourselves when the nuns did, and followed the prayers in the church prayer book. The only thing we did not do, as instructed, was go to communion. Sister Odonia told me that because I was not a baptized Christian, I could not go to communion. This was not yet a problem for my younger sisters.

I often returned to the convent from Sunday Mass feeling very angry. During some of his sermons, the priest expressed his sorrow for the tribulations suffered by the Jewish people in Belgium at the hands of the Nazis. But then he would say, with a sad expression on his face, that unfortunately today's Jews were paying for the sins of their fathers.

I could not understand why he started out by saying that he felt sorry for the Jewish people, then would say that they were paying for someone else's sins with their present suffering. When we returned to the convent, I would express my anger to Sister Odonia. "Why does he keep saying that we have to pay for the sins of our fathers? My father is a good man. My mother is a good woman. We are good people. We behave ourselves. He is wrong, and I wish he would stop saying those nasty things."

We remained hidden at the Franciscan convent in Doel for approximately three months. Then one day, Monsieur Ranson came to the convent to take us back to Brussels. We said good-bye to the nuns who gave each of us a hug and made us promise that some day, when the war ended, we would return for a visit. We had grown very fond of Sister Odonia and Sister Roberta and found it hard to leave. One consolation was that we were allowed to keep the slippers Sister Roberta had crocheted for us.

We went back to Brussels on the same flatbed truck, hidden under empty crates, in the same way we had been taken to Doel. When we asked Monsieur Ranson why we had to leave, he told us the Mother Superior was afraid to keep us any longer because it was becoming too dangerous. I was convinced that the reason we were obliged to leave was because Betty had drawn the Star of David and betrayed us, but I said nothing. I didn't want to upset my little sister.

Instead of returning us to the homes where we were hidden before leaving for Doel, Monsieur Ranson took us to our old apartment at 83 Rue François-Joseph Navez in Schaerbeek. Mama, Aunt Lea, Uncle Alex, and Nounou were still there and greeted us with hugs and tears. We were happy to be reunited, but it was difficult to be confined after having tasted freedom of movement in Doel. We slowly readjusted to the constraints of the apartment, though it now felt more crowded. Mama was still working at the factory, but did not return to the apartment every evening, often staying overnight, where she was helping the Belgian Resistance movement with some clandestine work.

Whenever she came back to us, she always brought us food that Monsieur Ranson had given her. We ate whatever Mama brought home whether we liked it or not. No one complained, not even Charlotte, was who normally a fussy eater. All we were interested in was assuaging our continual hunger. It was amazing that even Nounou, who was born in June 1940, just one month after the invasion, ate whatever was offered him. He somehow knew that he had no choice. He also knew instinctively that he had to be silent most of the time. If it was imperative for him to say something, he knew to whisper. He also knew that he could not make any noise whatsoever.

Once in a while, Mama would take our laundry to work with her because there wasn't enough water to wash it in the apartment. After a few days, she would bring back our clean clothes. It turned out that Monsieur Ranson was taking our laundry home and bringing it back to the factory after it was washed. I suspect that Madame Ranson probably washed the clothes, although it was never mentioned. Once in a while, Madame Fiers would do our laundry in her apartment, but we didn't want to trouble her too much as she was an elderly person.

Aunt Lea and Uncle Alex were concerned about Mama's safety, but Mama felt fairly safe wearing the crucifix the Ransons had loaned her and carrying her forged identity card.

It was wonderful to be with Mama, but approximately two weeks later, it was time for us to say good-bye to Mama and the family again. This time we were going to be hidden in a Catholic orphanage administered by the Sisters of the Order of Saint Joseph at 29 Rue des Champs in Etterbeek, a suburb of Brussels on the opposite side of the city. At least it was not as far away as Doel had been. Of course, this was again all made possible by Monsieur Ranson.

CHAPTER 8

Père Bruno

Through Monsieur Ranson Mama had made the acquaintance of Dom Bruno Reynders, or Père Bruno (Father Bruno), as we came to know him. Père Bruno was a monk, a member of the Order of Saint Benedict, who was a scholar and expert on early Christian writings, as well as a teacher. During the war he became an expert liar, thief and forger, with the kinds of expertise he needed in his second "career" as a rescuer of Jewish children and adults being hunted by the Gestapo. Père Bruno provided hiding places and stolen or forged identity cards to Jews that allowed them to pass as Aryans, as non-Jews. He also provided forged food ration cards to children and adults. Each card bore the *nom de guerre* of the individual and the imprint of a stolen municipal stamp to make them look authentic.

Père Bruno kept the food ration cards for the children and each month stood in a queue at the designated location to wait his turn and receive the month's allocation of food ration stamps. Without these cards, you starved. Most of the time, Père Bruno worked independently, but there were times he collaborated with others. After collecting the stamps, Père Bruno delivered them to different locations across the country where "his children," those he rescued, were hidden.

Early on a cold winter day in 1943, Mama took the three of us to the St. Joseph's orphanage in Etterbeek on a trolley car. It was raining, which was suitable weather, for it matched our moods, so dark and gray. We would have preferred to take a taxi to avoid the crowds standing in the rain waiting for the trolley car, but we couldn't take the risk because if we did, the taxi driver would know where we were going. What if he suspected us of being Jewish? Luckily, we did not have to wait long for the trolley and no one stopped us to ask for documents.

We held our breath a few times whenever German soldiers were around, and they were usually everywhere. One even took the trolley we were on and others were present at two trolley stops where we waited to transfer to connecting trolleys. One German soldier even smiled at us, and we sweetly smiled back. When we arrived at our destination, we faced an old, somber looking building with a heavy, wooden double-door. A chain hung to the right of it. When Mama pulled a few times, the sounds of a ringing bell reached our ears.

Soon enough, the heavy door opened and a nun with a kind smile (we later learned her name was Sister Egide) invited us to enter and led us to a room where we waited for the Mother Superior. When she came in and greeted us, Mama introduced us. She had nothing more to say. The Mother Superior was expecting us, for Père Bruno told her we would be coming. Mama then spoke to the Mother Superior for a while and then had to leave. There we were, three little girls who had to say good-bye to Mama once more, not knowing when or if we would ever see her again. We hugged, we kissed, we cried, and then Mama left.

We were very unhappy in Etterbeek. It was very crowded because of the war. I suspected that some of the other children were Jewish, but nobody shared that information. The nuns at Saint Joseph's were very strict and discipline was rigidly imposed, probably because some of the children were "problem" children – some were often punished and even slapped when they did not behave.

We slept in a large dormitory lined with white metal beds separated by a few feet of space from each other. A clothing hook was centered in the space between each bed, and that was where we hung clothes when we changed into nightgowns. There were two toilets at each end of the dormitory, and the water in these toilets often spilled over, flooding the floor around the cabinets and creating a bad, unpleasant odor. Between the toilet cabinets stood white, metal sinks, where each morning we brushed our teeth and washed our faces before we went downstairs to the refectory for breakfast.

The refectory was a large, colorless hall with several long, narrow wooden tables flanked by backless wooden benches. We were squeezed tightly against each other to make enough space for each child. Breakfast usually consisted of watery, cooked oatmeal. Sometimes they gave us bad-tasting, pale scrambled eggs with a small piece of bread. Lunch and supper consisted mostly of soup and potatoes with an occasional green vegetable tossed in. I didn't like the food and neither did my sisters. It was tasteless, but since we were always hungry, we ate it.

We understood, at least I did, that it was wartime and that food was rationed. The orphanage of Saint Joseph, which sheltered us, found it almost impossible to obtain enough food stamps to adequately feed all the children. Père Bruno provided the food stamps and payment for the children he took under his wing, but there were many other children at Saint Joseph's, who were not placed there by him. It was entirely possible that there weren't enough food stamps or sufficient funds to pay for everyone.

I was assigned to kitchen duty because I was one of the oldest children there. I peeled potatoes, washed vegetables and washed dishes, which I intensely disliked. Working in the kitchen had its advantages. When peeling potatoes or cleaning vegetables, I was able to slip potato peels and pieces of vegetables into my apron pockets. I sometimes even managed to steal a whole potato or two. When I would leave the kitchen, I would put my hands in my pockets over the potatoes so that the round protrusions would be my hands, not the potatoes. I shared these treasures with my sisters and Betty especially enjoyed them because she was always hungry. Before the war, I never dreamed that there would be a day when I would consider potato peels or pieces of vegetable a rare delicacy.

Whenever they served us those terrible eggs for breakfast with the chunk of bread, we had options. We could gulp it down immediately or ration it and thus enjoy it over several days. I rationed mine. Charlotte rationed hers. Betty would eat her bread as fast as she could. When she was finished with her bread she wanted some of Charlotte's or mine. Feeling sorry for this little sister of mine, I always gave her some of my bread. Eventually I would take her bread also and dole it out to her slowly. But there was a problem with the bread. It was thick and dark and tasted doughy – as if it had not been baked enough. If it lasted more than a day, the bread first turned slightly hard, then softened again and developed something that looked like mold by the third day, but we did not care. It filled our stomachs.

The other children were hungry, too, so there was quite a bit of thievery going on. I kept our bread in my pocket and hid it under my pillow at night. But even this did not prevent sticky-fingered felons from trying to wrest the food from me. Often, as I tried to sleep, I would suddenly feel something pushing against my pillow under my head. I would sit up with a start and catch the culprit. Furiously, I would kick the would-be thief, who would then run back to her own bed. As a result, during those days in the orphanage, I slept badly because I had to be constantly on guard.

Once a week everyone had to take a bath. Different groups were assigned to different days. A large round tub was placed on a platform about three feet from the floor, at arms' height of the attending nuns. Two small stepladders were placed in front of the platform, and the children lined up to one side of the tub. The younger children were the first ones to be bathed. Two older children, of whom I was one, would stand at the other end holding large towels in their hands.

The nuns would stand at the tub with a bar of soap and a washcloth, waiting. One at a time, each child climbed the stepstool into the tub of water. The nun would quickly scrub the child clean. Then the child would step out of the tub onto the other stepstool, where he or she was dried by the towel holders. After several children had passed through the tub, the water turned gray and murky and the towels were no longer clean and dry. But the baths were given in that same tub of water until every child scheduled for that day was washed.

On the first day Charlotte was bathed at Etterbeek, she was smacked across the face, hard, because she refused to get into the tub of murky water. Then the nun picked her up and forcefully placed her in the tub. Charlotte cried to no avail. She was scrubbed down and dried. I was distressed. I wanted to help her, to console her, but was not allowed to go near her. I felt so helpless. Betty, who probably would not have entered the tub willingly either, saw how Charlotte was treated, so she meekly entered the tub of truly filthy water. Eventually so did I, the last to enter this disgusting tub, when there were no more children to be dried.

I was tempted to refuse to go into the water, but as the oldest of the three, and because I was responsible for my sisters, I could not do anything to jeopardize our stay at the orphanage. I knew if we behaved and obeyed all the rules, we could stay at Saint Joseph's and be safe. That was the primary goal, no matter what.

So later that day, when we were alone, I reprimanded Charlotte and tried to explain to her and Betty the importance of all three of us doing exactly what we were told to do, whether we liked it or not. I felt sorry for both of them because I felt same way. But at the same time, I understood I had a responsibility to keep them safe.

In Etterbeek there was yet another problem, one we had never dealt with before – head lice. This was very annoying. We itched. We scratched. The scratching caused our scalps to develop a painful burning sensation. The nuns were aware of the problem and tried to solve it. Every once in a while we would line up and they would wash our hair with a special solution designed to rid us of the lice. But the treatment was useless, though it burned our scalps. I was able to remove the nits (lice eggs) and some of the lice from my sisters' hair and this helped a little, but it was a painful procedure. I had to pull the nits off each individual hair. Those poor kids! They cried, "It hurts, it hurts!"

Betty developed sores all over her scalp, which became infected. I learned that sometimes lice burrow under the skin causing sores to develop. I could not remove my own lice and nits and Charlotte and Betty couldn't remove them for me either because they didn't know how. I solved the problem by offering one of the older children a piece of bread the size of my thumb for every ten lice or nits she removed from my head. She had to show me the lice or the nits, which I counted before I carefully measured out the promised piece of bread.

But this wasn't the only thing that added to our discomfiture at the orphanage. Whenever air raid sirens sounded, we ran into the cellar, which was always damp. Water seeped in whenever it rained and, if the rainfall was heavy, it would flood and attract rats. We were afraid of the rats; they would scurry away when we came down and then daringly came out to inspect those who had invaded their domain. Sometimes the rats even made their way up to our dormitory and had to be chased out.

The orphanage also held primary school classes for children from first grade through fifth. The older children, like me, who were twelve and older, did not attend classes. We helped with the kitchen chores, made the beds in the dormitory, swept, and were assigned many other chores.

About four months after coming to St. Joseph's, the Mother Superior came to fetch us and took us to the parlor reserved for visitors. She said that there was someone who came especially to visit us. Was it Mama? My heart started to beat faster in anticipation of giving her a hug and a kiss. I knew by looking at my sisters' faces, as we held hands while walking across the courtyard, that they also thought Mama had come to see us. But it was not Mama. It was Père Bruno.

I had never met Père Bruno before, and I didn't know he was the person responsible for our placement at St. Joseph's, but as soon as I saw him, I liked him. Père Bruno embraced each of us and talked with Mother Superior for a few moments. Then Mother Superior left us alone with Père Bruno, who asked how we were doing. He wanted to know if the nuns were kind to us, if we were comfortable, if we received enough food. I answered affirmatively to all his questions and motioned to my sisters not to say anything negative.

We asked him when we could see Mama, when she would come for a visit. We also asked Père Bruno when we would be able to rejoin Mama at the apartment in Schaerbeek. He explained why we couldn't rejoin Mama yet and why Mama could not visit us. He promised he would come again and would tell Mama we were well and that we sent our love. The Mother Superior soon returned to the parlor with another nun who was carrying a tray with a small teapot, two cups, and a plate of cookies to which our eyes were immediately attracted. We were permitted to take one cookie each and then were told to say good-bye to Père Bruno, to leave the parlor and rejoin the other children.

The winter of 1943 turned into spring, which then turned into summer. As young children, the fear of punishment did not always deter us from breaking the rules. Sometimes, even I forgot that I had to be the responsible one.

The orphanage was built around a courtyard, part of which was separated by a high metal fence. The fenced-in part contained a garden locked behind a gate, where there were two beautiful apple trees growing, their branches laden with the most appetizing, but still quite green apples. The branches hung low from the weight of the fruit. We looked longingly at those apples and imagined biting into them and tasting their juicy contents. It did not occur to us that if the apples were not ripe, they would not taste as good as we imagined. But the desire to eat the apples of these life-filled trees distracted us from the greater danger surrounding us.

One bright summer day, a group of us older girls noticed that there was no one in courtyard, so with the help of some of the other girls we climbed over the fence to get to the trees. But the top of the fence was finished with spikes, which caused quite a bit of pain when our bodies pressed against them.

The lure of the apples, however, overshadowed the pain. We picked the apples as quickly as we could, throwing them over the fence to the waiting children. A few of the apples found their way into the fairly large pockets of our own smocks. After a few minutes, afraid of being discovered, we tried to climb back over the fence. I was the last in the garden, with no one left to push me over the fence – and there were no footholds. I handed my apples to Betty and Charlotte through the fence spokes and tried to pull myself up, but I couldn't. It was not long before one of the nuns came into the courtyard. She became very angry when she saw we had entered the forbidden territory and had stolen apples.

Meanwhile, though the apples were not yet ripe and quite tart, the other children had already devoured them. The culprits, and I was one of them, were to be swiftly punished, but before punishment could be meted out, shrill sounds of an air raid cancelled the disciplinarian's plans. Everyone rushed into the relative safety of the dreaded cellar, where we stayed for quite a while until the "all clear" sounded. By then, the nun lost her desire to punish us, but reprimanded us sternly and extracted our promise never again to disobey the rules.

In the middle of August that same year, I was haunted by a recurring thought and could not sleep. I was old enough to know we were hiding because we were Jews, but I could not understand why there was something wrong with being Jewish, why we were criminals while people of other religions were not.

While I was preoccupied with these thoughts, a nun came to wake me and gently shook my shoulder. When I looked at her she placed her forefinger against her lips, showing me that I should not make any noise. Silently, she indicated in pantomime that I had to get dressed and pointed to my two sisters. I woke them and when we were ready, we followed her to the entrance foyer of the convent where a young woman and the Mother Superior waited for us.

Without a word being said, the nun, Sister Egide, and Mother Superior gave each of us a quick kiss on the forehead. We left the building and followed the young woman, whose name we never learned, through the dark streets, hugging the buildings until dawn. Then we took a trolley to Schaerbeek, to the apartment at 83 Rue François-Joseph Navez, where we were reunited with Mama, Uncle Alex, Aunt Lea and Nounou. Once she had delivered us, the young woman disappeared.

CHAPTER 9

Our Clandestine Guide

We spent the rest of the month of August and part of September in the apartment. Only Mama would leave the apartment, and we went back to our former existence of silence, staying away from the windows or the balcony at the back, using the chamber pot during the day, and so forth.

We learned from the Fiers about the worsening conditions for the Jewish people. Arrests were constant and people were being deported. Mama was still working at the Ranson factory and continued to bring food to the apartment, but now she rarely stayed with us. Every few days she would bring us food then return to the factory where she spent her nights to reduce the risk of being seen on the street. We rationed the food to last as long as possible because we never knew when Mama would come with a fresh supply. We depended on Monsieur Ranson's ability to obtain food on the black market for our daily fare.

The stress, the boredom, the fear and the cramped quarters eventually caused tension to start building up between us. Uncle Alex, Aunt Lea and Nounou had been confined to our small apartment for almost a year, and there were no indications that the war was going to end anytime soon or that the Nazis would ever stop their unrelenting hunt for the Jews. This confinement was very difficult to take, especially an active person with a gregarious personality like Uncle Alex. It was probably more difficult for him than for the rest of us. He had always been physically active, enjoyed playing soccer in the park and taking long walks with his brother, Adolph. He also missed playing his mandolin, something he'd done during every free moment in his old life.

Somehow, I thought at first that Aunt Lea had adjusted better than Uncle Alex, because I'd never heard her complain about anything. She always seemed gentle and pleasant while she cared for the three of us and her little Nounou, that wonderful little three-year-old. But Aunt Lea began to suffer from serious depression and was convinced the Gestapo would catch us all, that there was no escape. This thought engulfed and overwhelmed her, no matter how much Mama tried to instill courage and hope in her.

Uncle Alex said nothing. His spirits were low, too, and his patience had worn thinner than tissue paper. As time passed, he became more and more impatient and difficult to live with. I tried not to irritate him. I kept busy, quietly helping Aunt Lea with the household chores, drawing and reading, when I was not playing with Nounou.

Charlotte was the most tranquil. She could sit quietly in one spot and observe everything and everyone, but little Betty was restless. She talked back to Uncle Alex when he told her what to do. One day she hit a raw nerve by going out on the balcony, something that was dangerous to do during the day, and was forbidden. Aunt Lea motioned to her to come inside and Betty refused. Uncle Alex also motioned to her to come back in and she refused again. Finally, he went outside, pulled her indoors, and without saying a word, put her over his knee and gave her a real spanking. She whispered that it did not hurt, so he hit her a little harder to extract her promise that she would be more obedient. He explained it was dangerous to go out on the balcony during daylight, but she would not promise. She was defiant and whispered again that it did not hurt. By the time Aunt Lea got him to stop hitting Betty, her buttocks were very red and looked inflamed, yet Betty never cried out. The only sign of distress she showed were tears that ran silently down her cheeks.

Then Uncle Alex realized that he had lost control and had forgotten that he was dealing with a seven-year-old, living under totally abnormal conditions. He put his arm around Betty and while hugging her, repeated several times, "I'm sorry, I'm sorry ... forgive me." This was the only time I ever saw Uncle Alex lose his temper with us.

When summer was over, we had to move again. We knew that Mama was in touch with Père Bruno through Monsieur Ranson and that Père Bruno was making arrangements to shelter us in a safer place. We did not know when the move would take place or where we would go. On September 23, 1943, Mama told us we would be leaving the following morning – she stayed with us overnight and we were delighted to spend the night curled up close to her, vying for the best spot.

Mama woke us gently at dawn and told us to get dressed, motioning for us to be very quiet, something that was part of our daily existence. After we were dressed, Mama gave each of us a piece of bread thinly spread with marmalade. Aunt Lea and Uncle Alex woke up and got out of bed to say good-bye, hugging and kissing each one of us and saying that we would soon see each other again. Aunt Lea repeated a few times that the war could not possibly last much longer and that everything would soon be over.

We took one last look at Nounou, who was still asleep. Aunt Lea's last words to us, as we walked out the door, were that as soon as the war was over, the family would once again be happy together. We didn't realize that this was the last time we would see our beloved aunt, uncle and cousin.

This time, Mama did not know where or with whom we would be hidden. She simply trusted Père Bruno. Those who offered us shelter also extended this offer to Nounou, but Aunt Lea and Uncle Alex would not accept. They were afraid to entrust their child to someone they did not know, to send him to a place unknown. They were well aware that the situation was becoming more and more precarious with each passing day, and that one day someone might suspect that Jews were hiding in the apartment and betray them to the Gestapo. But it was also dangerous to accept an offer of a hiding place for a child precisely because there were betrayals. No matter which way one turned, danger lurked. Mama decided to take that risk, but Aunt Lea and Uncle Alex did not.

Mama's instructions came from someone she knew only by a code name. She was told where and when to deliver us and was provided with a description of the person to whom she would hand us over. This person would then bring us to our hiding place. None of us knew where we were going, not even Mama. It was kept from us as a security measure, and Mama felt she had no choice but to trust Père Bruno and those who were willing to help us. Since going into hiding was becoming routine, we didn't ask questions. We were growing up. I was thirteen, Charlotte was ten and Betty was seven – we knew how to behave, how to signal each other, how to cause distractions.

We walked to the Gare du Nord because taking the trolley was too dangerous. Mama walked in front of us and we followed behind as if we didn't know her. We carried no suitcases, no bags, nothing, and arrived at 8 a.m., as instructed. We headed to the assigned platform to meet our traveling companion.

We'd said our tearful goodbyes in the apartment, hugging and kissing Mama as if our hearts would break. Now, recognizing the person we were supposed to meet, we were ready to walk away from Mama as if she were just a stranger waiting for a train. Our traveling companion was a woman of average height and weight with medium brown hair. She wore a dark blue suit and white blouse with a white handkerchief embroidered in light blue thread tucked into her breast pocket, exactly as described.

Mama stood to our left, a few feet away. The woman who would escort us stood to our right, also a few feet away. I stood still holding Charlotte's hand on one side and Betty's on the other while I stared straight ahead. I was tempted to turn to Mama, to hug her – my sisters wanting to do the same – but we dared not, fearing for our very lives.

About fifteen minutes later, the train rolled into the station, literally grinding its brakes until it came to a complete halt. The train doors opened and passengers disembarked, and when they were gone, the conductor invited the people waiting on the platform to climb aboard. The lady in the dark blue suit walked to the train, mounted the steps and entered a car. We followed her, exactly as we had been told to do. I had to help Betty, because she was too short to manage the stairs. The woman entered a compartment and sat down, so we followed her and sat down on the bench facing her. We did not speak to her, as we were instructed not to speak unless she spoke first. We looked out the window and could see Mama still standing on the platform. We caught her eye for just a second, and then, as the train slowly started to move, we watched Mama turn and walk toward the exit.

We sat quietly, still holding hands, waiting for the lady to speak. She did not, but once in a while, a subtle fleeting smile appeared on her face. We did not dare smile back. The train traveled through the beautiful Belgian countryside, the fields flowing peacefully by the train's windows. The train made several short stops at small, open-air railroad stations, but as long as our companion did not move, we silently sat and waited. Eventually the train stopped in Ruiselede, a small station that resembled many of the others in the countryside. The lady who had come for us then rose and left the compartment. As soon as she exited, we followed her off the train and out of the station for several meters. It occurred to me that we still had not exchanged a single word. Were we following the wrong person? Maybe she was not the one. What would we do if she wasn't the right person? Just as these thoughts raced through my frightened mind, the lady turned around, spread open her arms and said, "Don't be afraid, *mes petites* (my little ones), I'm taking you to a safe place."

I said nothing, but heaved a sigh of relief.

We continued to follow her, maintaining our silence. Charlotte and Betty held my hands. I noticed a street sign that read Bruggestraat. I also saw a church with a tall tower and steeple where Bruggestraat began. My eyes took in other sights as we walked along the streets of this charmingly quaint town. I would probably have enjoyed these sights at a different time, but right then I was filled with fear of the unknown and saw the same fear reflected in the eyes of my two little sisters. None of us knew what to expect in this new hiding place. We still had great difficulty grasping why we were the ones who had to hide. This hiding was serious hiding, not the childish game of hide and seek we used to play before this terrible war began.

Once again, the three of us found ourselves standing in front of heavy wooden double doors with a bell pull. The top of these doors was curved into an arch and they were as beautiful and polished as the building they graced. Madame Vanderveken, whose name we later learned, rang the bell and waited. A young, beautiful nun, Sister Jeanne Marie, opened the door and greeted us. We'd learned at the convent of the Sisters of the Order of St. Francis in Doel and at the orphanage of the Sisters of St. Joseph in Etterbeek that nuns were regular people, so by this time we knew there was nothing to be afraid of from a nun. We liked Sister Jeanne Marie immediately. The Sister guided us through a long, dim quiet corridor with high ceilings to a waiting room. As we walked we could hear the sound of our footsteps echo back to us. At our destination, she asked us to sit down and told us that she was going to fetch the Reverend Mother (the Mother Superior), who would be with us shortly.

The Reverend Mother, Marie Chrysostoma, was an imposing figure in her black habit and white starched collar and forehead band. She greeted Madame Vanderveken then nodded her head and smiled at us. We hesitantly smiled back, not yet completely reassured because, though everyone seemed kind, we did not know what to expect in this new, strange place we later learned to be the convent of Our Lady of Seven Sorrows.

Then again, when the Reverend Mother spoke to us, her face reflected such gentleness and kindness that we finally began to relax. Our first impression of her was later confirmed by her continued gentleness and kindness toward us and by her vigilant concern for our safety throughout the thirteen-and-a-half months we spent at her convent. Then the Reverend Mother and Madame Vanderveken exchanged a few words.

After Madame Vanderveken was served some coffee and cake by Sister Jeanne Marie, she prepared to leave so that she could return to Brussels before nightfall and the curfew. She said good-bye, told us that she would tell Mama we had arrived safely at the convent, and that we were in good hands. She admonished us gently to be good, to be obedient, and to be careful not to give ourselves away, but there was really no need for her to tell us that. By this time, young as we were, we knew that our lives depended on our behavior and recognition of the precarious situation we were in. I never forgot the way Mama impressed upon me that my safety, and that of my two sisters, depended on me.

Madame Vanderveken kissed each of us on the cheek and left.

We stood quietly, looking at each other, waiting to see what would happen next. Soon another nun walked into the waiting room, and the Reverend Mother introduced her as Sister Marie Consolata. She gave Sister Marie Consolata some instructions and asked us to follow her through the same dim corridor we had walked through upon our arrival. We turned into a corridor lined with large glass panes that allowed bright sunlight to stream in from the courtyard at the center of the convent buildings.

We followed Sister Marie Consolata up a flight of stairs to the second floor and entered a large dormitory. Several windows overlooked a small courtyard covered with a carpet of deep green grass. The windows faced another set of windows directly across from those of the dormitory. We discovered later that those windows were the sleeping quarters for the nuns.

Our dormitory held several rows of white metal beds, each one separated from the other by a night table. On each night table stood a bowl holding a pitcher, a soap dish with a piece of soap and a cup that held a toothbrush and toothpaste. A towel bar on the side of the night table held a towel.

Sister Marie Consolata told us about the dormitory rules. When we finished washing up every morning, we had to refill the pitcher with water for the next morning. Each of us was given a chamber pot to use during the night and we were told to place it under our beds. We were also shown how and where to empty and wash out the pots every morning. She also showed us where we would bathe once a week. As we looked around and listened to her instructions, we noticed one part of the dormitory was separated by a set of drawn draperies that closed it off from the rest of the dormitory.

I asked Sister Marie Consolata what the space was for and she told us that that was where the nun assigned to supervise the dormitory slept. Before we left the dormitory, she told us that later in the day we would each get a fresh set of clothes to wear the next morning.

Sister Marie Consolata then guided us through the rest of the convent, including our new living quarters. The refectory on the ground floor had long wooden tables with benches. Approximately thirty-five other girls of various ages were sitting on those benches, eating silently. Talking was not permitted.

We were assigned seats at one of the long tables and were served lunch. Lunch was actually dinner, a European custom. We timidly sat and ate. When the meal was over, the children left the refectory to play in the courtyard for twenty minutes before they returned to their classrooms. We did not go with them.

When we finished our meal, Sister Marie Consolata took us to the classroom to meet our teacher. One teacher taught all thirty-five children, who were at different levels of their primary school education. She divided the girls into small groups, teaching one group while another worked on an assignment. The few older children, like me about thirteen years old, were assigned to help the younger pupils with their writing and arithmetic exercises. We also performed duties that did not involve academic work.

We darned socks and also had some dormitory and kitchen duties. I soon learned that we were lodged in a temporary summer Fresh Air Camp for poor city children that was part of the convent. The children came for three-month stays to give their mothers some relief, and never had visitors. After the three months were over, they went home and did not come back.

We learned that our section was one part of a fairly large complex. One part contained the private lodgings for the nuns themselves, their dining room, living room, bedrooms and library. A beautiful chapel, where daily mass was held, was located diagonally across the hall from the Mother Superior's office. Another section contained a regular boarding school for the daughters of the upper bourgeoisie.

The students at the boarding school attended a daily range of classes, each level taught by individual teachers, most of them nuns. These students' facilities were quite elegant compared to our temporary ones. Their dining hall faced the gardens. The students ate at small tables for six to eight people. The tables were covered with tablecloths and decorated with vases of flowers. In the boarding school dormitory, each student had her own private alcove with a bed, a night table with bowl and pitcher, a desk and a small clothes closet. The alcove also had draperies that could be drawn when the student wanted privacy. These students also had their own, separate courtyard.

When we arrived at the convent on September 24, 1943, another Jewish girl, Ruth Wallach, known as Renee Leroy, was already there. She had arrived on September 13. Another Jewish girl, Paula A. Zand, known as Paulette Sanders arrived on November 4. The three of us were thirteen years old. We soon realized that no one in the convent except for the Mother Superior knew that we were Jewish children hiding from the Gestapo.

At first Renee, Paulette and I were not aware that we were all Jewish and in hiding. Charlotte and Betty didn't know that either, but we eventually discovered the truth and it created an unacknowledged kinship between us. We never talked about it, though we sometimes looked at each other knowingly, saying wordlessly, "We know why we're here."

One day Paulette was gone. I noticed she was missing that morning when we got out of bed. At breakfast I looked around and could not find her. What had happened to Paulette?

The other children had not seen Paulette either. When I still did not see her at dinner time, I asked Renee if she had seen Paulette. She said no, and she wondered where she was, too. When I asked Sister Marie Amata if she knew where Paulette might be she told us gently that Paulette had returned to her family. I was sad Paulette was gone and kept trying to come up with a reason for her sudden departure. Perhaps she was returned to her family because she was always crying. She seemed to have difficulty adjusting to life in the convent. When I asked if she would be coming back, Sister Marie Amata said she did not know. But we never saw Paulette again and never learned what happened to her after her departure from Ruiselede.

As we went about our chores we looked longingly at the other side of the courtyard, toward the boarding school. I wanted so very much to attend a normal school and study in a regular classroom with a teacher assigned to my age group. I loved learning and was very frustrated at not being able to advance in my lessons. I also wanted to eat in that beautiful dining room at a table covered with a tablecloth. I dreamed of having my own private sleeping alcove, or at least one that I would have to share only with my sisters.

CHAPTER 10

Ruiselede

One day, I approached the Reverend Mother Marie Chrysostome with a request to attend the boarding school. She explained that this was not possible because my sisters and I were not baptized Christians and could not go to communion when we attended Mass in the convent chapel. This was something we already knew, and when we attended Mass we stayed in our pew when the other attendees rose to make their way to the altar. But, I thought, as the Reverend Mother continued to speak, what does that have to do with our attending the boarding school? She explained. Not attending communion did not matter for my little sister, Betty, but it mattered for Charlotte and me. We were already at the age where we were required to go to communion. Not taking communion would catch the attention of other children in the chapel during Mass.

Children in the Fresh Air Camp did not receive visitors. They came, stayed the three months and then left. At the boarding school, the students stayed the entire school year, interrupted only by short vacations, one between the Christmas and New Year's holidays, and the other for the Easter holiday. The only long absence for the students was summer vacation between the end of June and the beginning of September. The students at the boarding school who noticed that we did not go to communion might possibly discuss this with family members who came to visit on Sunday afternoons. Therefore, she said, it was safer for us to stay in the Fresh Air Camp part of the convent.

I was very disappointed, but I knew she was right. That night I could not sleep. The same thoughts kept haunting me. Why did we have to hide? What were we guilty of? Why did those in charge of our country pursue us in order to arrest us and imprison us? What did my little sisters ever do to deserve this? Why could we not stay with Mama? Why did we have to keep moving from place to place? Mama had explained to me that being Jewish meant being subjected to antisemitism with all the difficulties that this entailed. However, she had continued, "Do not worry, God will protect you; you just do your part. Watch over your two sisters."

Apparently, Renee entertained the same thoughts I did. She also wanted to go to the boarding school, and realized that in order to do so she would have to convert to Catholicism. She was baptized and shortly thereafter was transferred to the elegant boarding school. In many ways, this severed our friendship, because now Renee was a boarding school student, attending classes and wearing the uniform that meant she was a member of the elite class of young girls residing in the convent, unlike us other poor girls, the charity cases accepted as guests for a three-month stay in the Fresh Air Camp.

Once in a while, when Renee and I would see each other when crossing the courtyard in the convent complex, she would hardly acknowledge me. I knew that if my sisters and I were baptized, we could also move to the boarding school. But this was out of the question. Mama's strict instructions before we left prevented me from even considering this. Mama had taken me aside once more and reminded me again of my responsibilities, so life continued to be difficult.

I was constantly torn between being a child myself and having to act as surrogate mother and caretaker for my sisters. The fear that the children might accidentally betray themselves, that if something were to happen to the two of them I would have to answer to Mama, kept me in a constant state of panic. When I could not sleep during the night and fear overtook me, I sometimes did not know whether I was more afraid of being caught by the Gestapo or having to face Mama. Because of this fear, I was very strict with my sisters, and they, in turn called me the *stepmother*. They formed a bond from which I was excluded. It saddened me, but I could do nothing about it. I had to follow Mama's orders for the sake of our safety.

We quickly adapted to our new surroundings and functioned well within the convent's routine and regulations. We had already acquired some experience in how to behave in a convent, and on the surface we looked no different than any other children. Betty and I resembled our mother, who had a very fair complexion. Charlotte, on the other hand, favored our father and was just slightly darker than we, as if she had a light suntan. This caused occasional concern but never became a problem.

One night, while sleeping, I was awakened by something pressing against my arm and the sound of a low plaintive whimpering: "Flora, I'm sick, I'm hurting." It was Charlotte. I sat up and she took my hand and guided it up to her neck and face where she felt the pain. As I lightly touched the side of her face I could easily feel the swelling. I did not know what it was, but I knew it was not good. I was worried and afraid, but I did not dare awaken the nun in charge of the dormitory during the middle of the night.

I helped Charlotte climb into my bed and held her in my arms until morning. By morning, Charlotte's face was even more swollen. I took her over to the nun in charge of the dormitory. Apparently there was little she could do for my poor little sister. She told her to stay in bed, and I was allowed to stay with her in the dormitory. After the other children had made their beds and said their morning prayers, the nun took them to the refectory for breakfast, while Charlotte and I stayed in the dormitory. When I placed my hand on Charlotte's forehead, it felt very warm. It was probably the fever which accompanied the mumps, which the nun suspected was the case because the other children had already had them. Professional medical care was out of the question.

I forced Charlotte to drink glass after glass of water, for I had learned from Mama that this was a way to bring down a fever. A nun occasionally relieved me so I could go down to the refectory to eat, though I did not want to leave my sister. After two days, I was told to attend to my chores. Although I did not want to, I had to leave Charlotte alone in the dormitory. This upset her very much, but after a period of several days she started to feel better and the swelling began to go down. Finally, after almost a week, the fever abated and Charlotte was on the road to recovery.

Betty, who was only seven years old when we arrived at Our Lady of Seven Sorrows, had some difficulty adjusting. By the time we left for Ruiselede, we had already been hidden in several places including the other two convents, but this time it seemed to be more emotionally difficult for all three of us, especially for Betty. The few weeks we spent with the family in Schaerbeek made this separation more difficult. It seemed to us that our lives consisted of mostly reunions and separations. The same question, like a refrain, always dominated our thoughts each time we parted: Will we ever see each other again? It was very difficult to leave other family members for the same reason.

Charlotte was always quiet, keeping her emotions to herself, but Betty acted them out. She did not always follow the rules and was often punished. I tried to intercede with the nuns but was told that discipline was important. I tried to explain to Betty why it was so important that we be very obedient. I explained again and again that if we did not obey they would not keep us and protect us from those who wanted to find and hurt us, though I knew it was difficult for someone as young as Betty to truly comprehend the danger. I myself did not understand why, but what I did understand was that our lives were threatened so we could not inadvertently let anyone know that we were Jewish.

At night I thought about many things, mostly about our extended family members from Antwerp, who were close to us even though we were not actually related, like Jackie, my idol, and his younger brother, Harreke. I thought about Heleneke and her older brother, Louis, and Nounou, whom the three of us loved so much, and his parents. I thought about the family members in far away Romania – our grandparents and all the aunts and cousins there, and wondered what was happening to them.

Mama was never far from my thoughts. It was as if a long line of people, their faces imprinted in my mind, moved continuously before me. Were they safe? Where were they now? Finally I would fall asleep, but when I opened my eyes again, it was morning, bright daylight would stream through the windowpanes, and it was time to rise and start a new day – in hiding, following the same routine, as always.

I said good morning to my sisters, gave each of them a hug, then helped Betty wash and dress. Charlotte washed and dressed herself. The other children in the dormitory did the same and then we all made our beds and followed Sister Marie Amata, a gentle and kind soul, to the refectory for breakfast, where we prayed and ate. Breakfast was not luxurious, but it was adequate considering it was wartime. We were fortunate to be at Our Lady of Seven Sorrows – we weren't always hungry because there was enough food. The convent had its own gardens and fields where they grew vegetables and potatoes. There was even an orchard where a variety of fruit was grown.

Breakfast was followed by a short recess in the courtyard and then we would go to the classroom where the teacher – who was not a nun – waited for us. As we filed in, she rose from her chair, greeted us, and led us in prayer after we were seated. It always felt strange having to say Christian prayers about Mary and Jesus, but we did. But as I recited prayers alongside the other children, I silently talked and prayed to God and asked Him to forgive my sisters and me for praying in another religion. I told Him, as if He didn't already know, that we had no choice. I also asked Him to end the war so we could return to Mama and be free.

As I described earlier, the teacher checked the older girls' assignments first and then the older girls helped the younger girls. I did not always stay until the end of the class because I had other chores to attend to. I was taught to darn socks, repair small tears and was asked to sew on buttons that had come loose. Sometimes I washed the dishes and helped set the tables in the refectory for mealtimes. When I was free, the Reverend Mother, Marie Chrysostome, permitted me to go into the convent library and read to my heart's content, but only in the library. I was never allowed to remove any books from that room. I always found it hard to leave the library without reaching the end of a story and could not wait to return. As soon as I finished one book, I was ready to start reading another.

While in Ruiselede, I read hagiographies and became acquainted with the lives of many saints. When reading, I could forget the world around me and why I was in a Catholic convent. I knew that on some level the Sisters were placed in danger when their Mother Superior had agreed to shelter us, yet I did not completely understand the extent of that danger. Later, I found out the penalty for sheltering a Jewish person, child or adult, was immediate death or incarceration as a slave laborer in a concentration camp, where many died long and horrible deaths.

In Brussels we had had to speak in French, but in Ruiselede we were back in a Flemish-speaking region and could once again speak in the language of our childhood. The convent library contained books in both languages, but most of the books were Flemish. Thus, without being conscious of it, I improved my skills in Flemish and French.

Although Ruiselede was a small town in the countryside, it was not spared war planes flying overhead, screeching sirens, bombing and shooting. Here, too, we regularly had to run to the cellar to be protected from bombs and strafing. During one raid, Sister Marie Amata was hit in the leg by shrapnel that left her with wounds that never totally healed.

Most of the time I obeyed the rules, but sometimes, when I felt too confined, I would sneak out without telling anyone, not even my sisters. I would head for a nearby field where wheat was growing, gracefully waving back and forth in the gentle breeze, and make my way into the middle. Once there, I would sit down and be hidden from anyone's view. I would sit there just looking up at the sky, savoring a sense of imaginary freedom and peace.

Sitting there, I would think about how wonderful life was before the war began. I remembered our outings before Papa left for America. We often visited the Rubens Museum, where Mama would explain to us why some things that people made were called "art." Mama loved classical music and occasionally took us to a concert. We attended the Yiddish theater that was very popular. We would visit Nightingale Park outside of the city, where Mama taught me how to pick mushrooms. She showed me how to recognize the edible ones from those that were poisonous. I also daydreamed about our summertime visits to Belgian resorts like Knokke or Blankenberg.

Sitting there in the field, I watched birds flying, and as my eyes followed their wings, the pleasure of my temporary freedom faded. I would ask myself, as I had done many times before, "Why must we hide? Why must we conceal our identity using fake names? Why must we hide our Judaism? Why? Why? What did we do to deserve this?" At that moment, I wished I were a bird so I could be free and fly whenever and wherever I wished. After a few minutes, I would reluctantly get up and return to the confines of the convent, praying and hoping that no one had noticed my absence.

No one ever did.

One time I came back and was walking down the hallway that faced the garden where the statue of the Virgin Mary stood, trying to make my way without being seen, when, unexpectedly, I came face to face with Sister Marie Renata and Sister Marie Modeste. The two nuns greeted me with a friendly smile and continued on their way. I let out a sigh of relief, and then headed for the refectory to do my chores.

While most of the nuns in the convent were unaware that my sisters and I were Jews, I think that a few, like Sister Marie Consolata, Sister Marie Amata, and Sister Jeanne Marie, suspected the truth and never said a word. Sometimes I wondered why the Reverend Mother sheltered us so willingly and risked her life and the lives of the other nuns in the convent. I learned that the Sisters of the Order of Our Lady of Seven Sorrows had been opening their

doors to war refugees and wounded military personnel since their establish-
ment 300 years earlier. When I saw elderly people in the convent, I learned
that these nuns also took in and cared for older people who could not take care
of themselves.

In addition to the boarding school for upper middle class girls and the
Fresh Air Camp for poor city children, the nuns administered a parochial day
school for the children of Ruiselede. The principal of the day school was a
nun we called *La Directrice* – I never learned her real name. On the surface
she gave the appearance of being very stern, but we soon realized she was
really quite gentle and kind. I asked the Reverend Mother if we could attend
the day school. She said no, and explained that it would be too risky because
the children who attended that school returned home every day and it would
seem strange that three girls who lived in the convent would be attending their
school and not the boarding school. It could be dangerous if they shared this
information with their families.

We stayed at the Ruiselede convent during 1943-1944, while the war
raged on. By now the war was not going so well for the Germans. German
soldiers were starting to defect. The convent received sporadic visits from
German officers and Gestapo looking for criminals, like German soldiers who
went AWOL, escapees from POW camps and Jewish people in hiding. When
the doorbell rang and a nun looking through the peephole saw a man in uniform, she would immediately notify the Mother Superior instead of opening
the door. The Mother Superior would then assign one of the nuns to take Charlotte, Betty and me down to one of the storage cellars.

After a while the nuns no longer needed to be told what to do or why.
They knew. The worst of these incidents occurred one day as we had to rush
down to the cellar that stored heaps of potatoes, apples and other produce
grown on the convent's farm. We hid, with the Sister, behind a large pile of
potatoes, practically holding our breath. Not long after we settled ourselves
on the concrete floor behind the pile, we heard the cellar door open and heavy
footsteps descending the steps. Then a harsh voice shouted in German: "Is
anybody here? Out! Out! Is anybody here? Out! Out!"

From the footsteps we knew there was more than one person. We heard
them walking back and forth and kept very quiet. The nun had her arms around
Betty's waist. We heard fruit and/or potatoes rolling off other piles in the cellar. Then, suddenly we heard the potatoes rolling from the front of our pile.

Everything stopped and there was total silence for a minute or two. Finally, we heard the footsteps going toward the cellar steps, mount them, and leave. We sat. None of us moved. We waited for what seemed like hours. Finally, the nun said she thought that we were safe and we could leave. She took us for a short walk, giving us time to calm down and relax. Then she accompanied us to the kitchen where she gave us each a cup of milk, let us sit for a while, and took us back to our section of the convent. Before taking her leave, she gently reminded us not to tell anyone where we had been.

CHAPTER 11

Mama Comes To Stay

I was not worried when Reverend Mother Marie Chrysostome called me into her office in May 1944. Occasionally, Mama was able to smuggle a letter to us via underground courier, but not very often. When such did letters arrive, the Reverend Mother would have it brought to us or she would call us to her office and personally hand-deliver it. I did think it unusual, however, that this time she had asked me to come get the mail without bringing my sisters along.

I knocked on the Reverend Mother's office door and her soft voice invited me in. She asked me to sit beside her and read the letter she handed me out loud, a very unusual request. I read:

> My dearest Flora,
> I hope this letter finds you and the children well. I miss the three of you very much. I wish I could have you with me, but I am sure that you know and understand that this is not possible. With this letter, I want to tell you that Aunt Lea, Uncle Alex and Nounou went away on vacation to visit the rest of the family. I do not know when they will return and in the meantime I do not know what to do. Stay well, my darling, and continue to take care of the children.
> Kiss both children for me.
> Mama.

When I finished reading the letter to her, the Reverend Mother asked me to interpret what Mama wrote. "I think," I responded, then hesitated for a moment before continuing, "that Mama is telling me that our Aunt Lea, Uncle Alex and our little cousin, Nounou were caught by the Gestapo."

As soon as I said that, the tears welled up in my eyes and began flowing down my cheeks. Without saying a word the Reverend Mother handed me a handkerchief and gave me a few minutes to regain my composure. She then handed me a sheet of writing paper and a pen.

"What should I do with that?" I asked.

"You will write your mother a letter which I will dictate," was her reply. I was puzzled. She had never dictated any letters I had written to Mama before, so why would she do so now? But she was the Mother Superior; I did what I was told to do. I leaned forward over the desk, pen in hand, and waited. She started:

> Dear Mama,
> I received your letter. We are all fine. Mama, I have a great idea. While Uncle Alex, Aunt Lea, and Nounou are away visiting the rest of the family, you must come here to visit us. That way you will not be by yourself until they return. I cannot wait to see you and I am sure it is the same for the children. We send you many kisses from all of us.
> We love you,
> Flora

When I was done writing the letter, the Reverend Mother told me to return to the other children and my regular duties. She suggested I say nothing to my sisters about uncle Alex's family and their probable faith. She also told me not to say anything about the invitation to Mama and the possibility that she might come to stay in the convent. When I got back, my sisters asked me where I had been. I told them that I was in the Mother Superior's office, but did not tell them why. When they persisted wanting to know why, I told them that I had to help her rearrange some of the books in the library. This satisfied them. I disliked lying to my sisters, but I did have to tell them something that satisfied their curiosity and stopped their questions.

The rest of the day passed uneventfully, except that I was in a turbulent emotional state. There were no air raids and no Germans coming to search the convent. But that night I could not sleep. I spent a restless night tossing and turning. Was Mama really going to come to Ruiselede to stay in the convent with us? Would we be able to see her and be with her? It seemed unreal. I was anxious to tell my sisters, so that they could enjoy the anticipation, but I was not permitted to share this information.

Beyond that, it hurt to know that the Gestapo had arrested and taken away our Nounou and his parents. What kind of monsters were those Nazis? Why did they do what they did? When all the children, including my sisters and me, kneeled at the side of our beds that evening to recite the evening prayers, I prayed to God to make sure Mama would be able to arrive safely at the convent, so that nothing should happen to her on the way to us. I was also very angry and expressed it silently to God, for I knew that He would know what I thought. I silently let Him know that He owed it to my sisters and me to bring our mother safely to the convent because He had allowed the other members of the family to be taken away.

The next few days passed uneventfully. Then, on a Wednesday morning, the Reverend Mother came to the courtyard during recreation time and asked the three of us to come with her. We followed her to her office. My heart started to beat rapidly. Was it…? I wanted to ask, but did not dare. It seemed that the hallway leading to the Mother Superior's office had quadrupled in length and took us much longer to get there than usual.

We walked in and the Reverend Mother pushed us ahead of her. My sisters and I saw the back of a sitting figure rise from the chair. The figure turned around. The three of us let out a scream, "Mama!" Then, continuing to scream "Mama, Mama…" we ran to Mama who was heading toward us with outstretched arms. We fell into her arms. Mama embraced us, looked at us with hungry eyes filled with love and kissed us again and again. We, in turn, could not stop kissing her and repeating, "Mama, we missed you so much." We had not seen Mama for seven-and-a-half months – an eternity.

I did not ask Mama anything about Aunt Lea, Uncle Alex or Nounou. I knew that she did not want the children to know. The Reverend Mother stood by and allowed us to get our fill of hugging and kissing each other. When she realized that we would never get our fill, she motioned for us to separate and sit down. We obeyed and sat down. Mama did also.

The Reverend Mother told us that Mama would be staying in the convent, but we could not be lodged with her. Mama would live in her own private room in a section of the convent reserved for adult residents. We three had to remain in our present section with the other children. She told us that she would come and fetch us once a week to visit secretly with Mama in her room for about one-half to three-quarters of an hour. We were also instructed not to reveal to the other children or to anyone else that Mama was our mother. There were already several other residents, all Christians, in the convent, so Mama's presence would not be seen as anything unusual.

Her Jewish identity had to be kept a strict secret as well. We were also told that should we occasionally, unexpectedly see Mama in one of the hallways, the courtyard, or the garden, we were not allowed to "recognize" her or speak to her. We had to pretend that we were not acquainted with her, that she was just one of the other residents who lived in the convent and who greeted us and smiled. We were allowed to politely greet Mama and smile back.

Before we knew it, it was time to part. We reluctantly separated ourselves from Mama and left to rejoin the other children.

As difficult as it was, we left Mama and the Mother Superior alone. Even little Betty, not quite grasping why, understood what she had to do and obeyed the orders we were given. It would be worth it to see Mama occasionally in the hallways.

As soon as we left her, we were already looking forward to our next visit. Despite the need to keep our distance from her, I felt a surge of happiness. Charlotte and Betty were also happy, knowing that Mama was nearby and we would see her soon. Though we were still in danger of being caught by the Gestapo, who were becoming more relentless in their pursuit of hidden Jews, we had at least one cherished gift: having Mama with us.

A few days after she settled into the convent routine, Mama approached the Reverend Mother and offered to work on the farm, in the orchard or anywhere there was a need for a worker inside the convent complex. She wanted to work because she needed cash to cover her expenses for lodging and food at the convent. Our expenses were taken care of by Père Bruno.

At first the Mother Superior declined to accept Mama's offer. She told Mama, addressing her as "*vrouw Fani*" (Mrs. Fani), that she was her guest and there was no need to be concerned about any payment. Mama was an individual who had great difficulty accepting a gift without giving something in return. She considered this charity, so she insisted. In addition, she also needed to be actively engaged in something. Upon Mama's insistence, the Mother Superior reluctantly allowed her to work in the orchard.

Mama's family had owned orchards when she was a young child in Romania, and the fruit of the trees provided the family's income. During the summer when she did not have to attend school, Mama and the other children in the family helped with the harvest, so Mama knew what needed to be done.

Every Sunday, immediately after lunch and just before Vespers in the chapel, we would happily go to Mama's room for an afternoon visit, albeit a short one. It was opposite the staircase to the nuns' sleeping quarters directly above on the second floor, that was also home to other adult residents. Situated near the double front doors leading out to the Bruggestraat, the main street of the village, the room was small and had a fairly large window, hung with a drawn heavy drape, looking out on the street. There was a bed, two chairs, two night tables, a medium-sized armoire and a narrow table to the left of the door that Mama used as a desk. As soon as the door was closed and we were alone with her, Betty would climb onto Mama's lap, and Charlotte would pull over a chair, sit down and hold onto Mama's arm. With the room's two chairs taken, I usually sat on Mama's bed. The first such visit came after Mama's first Mass.

The first time Mama came to the chapel for the Mass service, I was relaxed because when Mama asked me what she had to do when in the chapel I casually said, "Just watch the other people, Mama, and do what everyone else does. It is easy." I did forget one thing, however, the most important one. I forgot to tell her not to follow the others when they went up to the altar to receive communion.

The priest, the Reverend Jozef Van Rijkeghem, led the congregation in the ritual of the Mass while I, sitting or kneeling in my pew, realized that I had forgotten to tell Mama not to go to communion with the others. I was desperately trying to think of a way to warn her before the ritual was performed, but if I got up and went over to the pew where Mama was sitting, I would attract attention. I could not communicate with her by sign language for the same reason. Mama was sitting in a pew on the other side of the aisle from where the three of us were seated with the other children from our section. I had no choice but to wait and hope. The time for the offering of communion arrived. Worshippers throughout the chapel rose from their seats in the pews and began slowly to make their way down the middle aisle of the chapel toward the altar where the priest was waiting with two altar boys at his side.

Those at the front of the queue spread out and kneeled at the ornate wooden railing that spread from the center of the middle aisle across the width of both sides of pews. As I looked across the aisle, I was suddenly filled with fear as I saw Mama get up, exit from her pew and become part of the queue of worshippers heading toward the front of the chapel to receive communion. I knew that she didn't know what that was. I tried to make eye contact with her as she came down the aisle closer to the pew where my sisters and I sat with the other children. I did not succeed. Mama continued to make her way down the aisle, seriously holding her head bent and her hands clasped together, just like those who preceded her. I had one thought: we're lost.

I kept my eyes on Mama. She arrived at the railing in front of the altar where the priest stood holding the goblet containing the communion wafers. She kneeled just as the others did. When the priest approached Mama with the goblet in his hands, she tilted her head backwards, opened her mouth and waited. Nothing reached her mouth. She had closed her eyes. When she opened them the priest was already offering a wafer to the person kneeling next to her. She made the sign of the cross as she had seen others do before her, raised herself up from her knees, and slowly returned to her pew with her hands clasped. I was paralyzed with fear. What will happen now I asked myself. Fortunately, my suffering was in vain. Nothing happened.

During our early afternoon visit with Mama on that same day, I told her that I had forgotten to tell her not to go to communion. I also explained to her what communion meant. She replied that the priest had not placed anything on her tongue after he had said the preparatory prayer. She was sure, she said, that no one had noticed because the priest went through the entire ritual, preparatory prayers and all, short of offering her the wafer. Someone, however, had noticed.

A female worshipper kneeling next to Mama, was also waiting to receive communion, and noticed that the priest did not offer the wafer to Mama. After the Mass, she approached the Reverend Van Rijkeghem to ask him about her observation. He denied her accusation and told her that she was mistaken, that he had indeed offered Mama the communion wafer. He then admonished her by saying that if she was before him and the altar to receive communion, how come she was not concentrating on receiving the Lord instead of looking around and sinning by trying to find flaws in others. Of course, Mama learned her lesson well. She never again presented herself for communion.

The time we spent with Mama always seemed too short. No sooner did we relax and begin to enjoy our visit, when there would be a knock on the door and the Reverend Mother would tell us that it was time to go back to our section. As usual, we did not want to leave, but we had to. As the three of us walked back to our section that day, we met Renee in the hallway. I had not seen her for several weeks, except in the chapel at Mass. She walked quickly past us. Perhaps she was in a hurry, I thought. Perhaps, now that she was a Christian, she was not comfortable with us. I do not know why, but I felt sorry for her. I also felt lucky now that we had Mama close to us in the convent.

We continued on our way to join the other children and to prepare to attend Vespers in the chapel. The sounds of the choir voices reached us when we entered and sat down in our pews. I looked up and saw Mama in one of the pews on the other side. I was surprised. When I asked her about this later she said that she thought it would be wise for her to be seen at services other than Mass.

A Christian woman, a resident in the convent, befriended Mama. They took walks together, ate together in the civilian dining room, and generally spent free time together. The woman liked Mama – most people who met Mama liked her. As this woman became more familiar with Mama, she confided in her more and more. Mama, however, was careful not to reciprocate with confidences, except superficially. The woman hated Jews and anyone who was unlike herself, anyone who was not a Christian or a Belgian. She considered them all enemies. She constantly spewed hateful expressions against Jews: "Jews are dirty, Jews stink, they are thieves, they are sneaky, they have shifty eyes, they are evil...."

Mama tried to suggest that she might be wrong. She talked to her about this in a careful manner, in order not to offend her and not to betray herself. But this woman was filled with such a deep hatred that it frightened Mama.

June 1944 passed fairly uneventfully, and then on July 29, we celebrated Mama's thirty-eighth birthday in her room. The Mother Superior fetched us and stayed to share a birthday cake and give Mama a gift – a round, decorated tin box. We gave Mama our hand-drawn birthday notes and hugged and kissed her. We could not sing "Happy Birthday" because no one was supposed to know that we were visiting or that she was our mother. She suggested that Mama open the tin box. Mama did. The Reverend Mother knew that Mama loved cherries, something she must have learned from Mama in an earlier conversation. The box, graced with a white envelope, was filled with the first cherries of the season. Mama picked up the envelope, anticipating a birthday card or note. But when the Reverend Mother asked her to open the envelope, she found it filled with Belgian francs. Mama turned to the Reverend Mother, stretched out her hand and tried to return the envelope to her and said, "No, this is too much. You are sheltering my children. Now you have invited me to be sheltered here and you are also giving me gifts? I will accept the cherries, but I cannot accept the money. Please take it back."

The Reverend Mother refused and told Mama that she must keep it because the war would eventually end and this money would give us a head start until Mama was able to earn some on her own. Mama capitulated and kept the money, thanking the Mother Superior profusely. The three of us also chimed in with our thanks. The Mother Superior then left and told us that we could stay with Mama a little longer than usual because it was her birthday. We were delighted.

As the summer progressed, there was more military activity in the town. There were more German soldiers on the streets of the small village and more soldiers deserting the German army. The searches for those who went AWOL intensified and hardly a day went by without someone in uniform coming to ask if there were men seeking shelter. Those who helped deserters suffered a punishment that was swift and harsh.

In August of 1944 we were very busy running back and forth to the cellar because the sirens screeched more often. More airplanes flew over Ruiselede and we heard the distant thumps of bombs finding their marks. During one of those bombings, parts of the convent were hit, and many windows were shattered.

Even as the final battles of the war raged around us, we continued to function according to our regular routines, albeit with interruptions. Sometimes, in between the sirens and the bombings, we went out for walks in the countryside, beyond the center of Ruiselede. This was a rare occurrence, done to distract and relax the children from the stress of warfare.

Mama was not forbidden to leave the confines of the convent, if she wished to do so, and sometimes she did. She met a couple, the DeKosters, who sometimes attended Mass at the convent chapel with their children. They were unaware that Mama and her three daughters were living in the convent of the Sisters of our Lady of Seven Sorrows to hide from the Gestapo. Then

Charlotte befriended the DeKosters' daughter and the girls enjoyed playing together. During some of the rare longer visits we had with Mama, and unbeknownst to Mother Superior, we would visit the DeKoster home near the Bruggestraat, just a short distance away. We thoroughly enjoyed these stolen moments, when we felt free and almost normal by visiting a family at home. Of course, the DeKosters were completely unaware of the fact that we were Jewish, since all four of us were very competent and experienced actresses.

On August 16, 1944, I celebrated my fourteenth birthday. I did not know that being fourteen years old was to be young in years. Outside of a moment here and there, I felt old and joyless. The last time I experienced real happiness was on my ninth birthday, the last one we celebrated with many members of the family – Mama, my sisters, Uncle Alex, Aunt Lea, Nounou, our Jackie, Harreke, Heleneke, Louis, their parents and others. Even with Papa in America, it was still a happy day. Mama brought up the fact that it would have been a happier one if he had been present to share the celebration with us. She said, "We will soon be reunited in America with Papa and then every day will be a celebration."

About a week after my birthday, the Reverend Mother told us that Père Bruno had inquired about us. He wanted to know if everything was going well. Of course, she had said, we were fine and safe. I was sorry that he did not come for a visit. We loved him. He had such a calm, gentle way about him. When you were with him you had a feeling of total safety. He had such a wonderful way of reassuring us that we had nothing to fear. His face reflected this gentle kindness. Even if I could not see him or personally speak with him, I was pleased that he thought of us and had been concerned about our well being, as well as Mama's. He knew that Mama was with us because it was he who had given Mama the name and address of the convent as well as directions how to reach it.

CHAPTER 12

Liberation

On September 8, Ruiselede was caught in the crossfire between Allied and German troops who'd left Tielt and were fighting their way toward Ruiselede. Other Allied troops were coming toward Ruiselede from the other direction. The fighting and shooting lasted all day and the convent suffered much damage from this last battle.

The German troops fought hard and furiously, but finally, by evening of that historic day, they succumbed to the onslaught of the brave Allies. Our liberators were Polish fighters in exile in Great Britain who joined the British Forces to liberate Europe from the yoke of German occupation. All that day, we children, and the nuns who cared for us – like Sister Consolata, Sister Jeanne Marie, and Sister Marie Amata – sat huddled in the cellar as the shooting raged on. We waited for some time when the shooting stopped. Then, when one of the Sisters thought it was safe, we slowly ventured outside. When we reached the street we were surprised to see that we were not the only ones exiting shelters. The other nuns, boarding school students and the civilian residents of the convent, including Mama, were already in the street.

Most of the residents of the Bruggestraat and surrounding side streets shouted greetings to Allied soldiers who were sitting on top of tanks and other vehicles as they headed toward the church located at the end of the Bruggestraat. During the fighting, German snipers had positioned themselves in the church tower. Now, as our eyes followed the Polish soldiers riding toward the church, we saw a white rag hanging from it, signaling that the Germans had surrendered. The war, at least here, was over!

Young soldiers sitting on top of the tanks smiled and waved to us. We waved back vigorously with our arms swinging from side to side and shouted, "Welcome! Welcome!" An especially handsome young man sat on one of those tanks as it passed by us, smiling and waving. I guess I was at an age when I had started to notice those things. Suddenly we heard shooting again. It seemed to come from the church tower. The tanks swiveled around and headed back, retreating through the Bruggestraat. We didn't move. We all remained frozen in our places on the sidewalk. The tank carrying the handsome smiling soldier passed us by. The soldier was not waving. He was not smiling and he was not sitting. He was sprawled on top of the tank, blood oozing from his face and body. I was devastated.

How cruel was the enemy; how false were those soldiers in the tower. They betrayed the meaning of their white flag. They had lured the Allied troops toward them with their pretense of surrender only to murder those who had trusted the signal. Then the fighting started again but more furiously than before. All of us ran back to the cellars. When the sun went down and evening darkness covered the town, the shooting stopped again. This time the fighting was really over in Ruiselede. The German soldiers were taken prisoner and the Allied troops took over and occupied the town.

By the end of September most of Belgium was liberated. Mama soon planned our return to Brussels. Why Brussels and not Antwerp? Mama felt that most of the surviving family members who had fled to Brussels, where they were captured by the Gestapo, would most likely return Brussels to find out if other family members had survived the war's horrors. Brussels was to be our destination.

The Reverend Mother suggested we leave Charlotte and Betty at the convent until we found suitable lodgings, and we could come back for them. Mama agreed. My sisters were unhappy but Mama explained the difficulties of traveling under these post-war conditions and that there was no housing waiting for us in Brussels. Mama promised that as soon as we were settled, we would return to Ruiselede and bring them back with us. That seemed to satisfy them.

Travel was indeed very difficult. The trains did not run on a regular schedule and often not at all. Railway tracks were damaged in the fighting and so were many trains. Somehow we managed to catch a train to Tielt. From there we hoped to find a train going to Brussels, but we had no luck. None of the trains in working order were traveling in that direction, so we decided to walk, hoping we could hitchhike in that direction.

We also thought that perhaps a bus might be heading for Brussels and would stop for us. Finally, a canvas covered truck, part of a convoy transporting Allied soldiers, gave us a lift. We asked if their destination might perhaps be Brussels. They nodded yes, and helped us up into the truck. After we were settled, the truck continued on its way. We sat quietly. Once in a while a soldier would smile at us and we smiled back. Conversation beyond the most elementary words was out of the question.

Suddenly the entire convoy stopped. There was shooting, but we did not know where it was coming from. Everybody got off the truck and tried to use the truck as a shield, hoping it would protect us from bullets. One of the soldiers helped Mama and another one picked me up and handed me down to a soldier already standing on the pavement. We ducked to the ground just behind the truck. The shooting continued for a while and then stopped. When we stood up, a horrible sight faced us. One of the soldiers who had been with us lay flat on the pavement, his head tilted back to reveal a large deep cut that almost severed his head from his body. He was dead.

Though Mama and I had witnessed such things before, we were horrified anew each time. One just cannot get used to seeing such sights. As we looked around, we saw several other bodies strewn across the highway. Soldiers from our truck and others in the convoy picked up the bodies and placed them carefully in one of the trucks. Then we continued on our way. When we reached the outskirts of Brussels we thanked the soldiers, especially the driver who had stopped for us. The soldiers then continued to travel in another direction. We later learned that though the German Army in Belgium had officially surrendered, there were still pockets of resistance across the country.

We sat down on the side of the road, hoping to hitchhike into the city. To our great surprise, a public bus stopped right in front of us. We had not noticed we were sitting at the public bus stop. When we looked up, the sign said the stop was for buses going to Schaerbeek, and that was exactly where we wanted to go. The bus doors opened and we mounted the steps onto the bus, but not before Mama double-checked and asked the driver whether he was going to Schaerbeek. "Yes," he said.

Mama and I took our seats and looked out the window at the familiar sights. We heaved a sigh of relief. We could not believe that we were sitting in a public bus, traveling to a place of our choice, and not having to fear being arrested. What a wonderful feeling. It was indescribable. We were free! Nothing, for the moment, could diminish this joy of feeling free.

The bus dropped us off in Schaerbeek, close to Rue François-Joseph Navez. We walked to number eighty-three, the last place we had lived before dropping out of sight. We rang the bell to the Fiers' apartment. No one was home. We walked to the home of Monsieur and Madame Hotton. No one was there either. We passed a car repair shop whose owner we knew. We hoped he would be there to give us some information about the Hottons and the Fiers, and there he was, working on a car.

He greeted us warmly. We told him we'd just returned to Schaerbeek from the countryside where we had been hiding from the Nazis. He asked if we had a place to sleep for the night. When we said no, he offered us his office. He told us that he had two cots, pillows and blankets, which should be adequate for our needs. He also had several towels for us. He had these items in his shop because he sometimes stayed late when a repair order took longer than he anticipated.

We slept in the garage office for about two weeks. Then we learned that the American Jewish Joint Distribution Committee (JDC) had opened an office in Brussels to help Jewish survivors returning from hiding places and survivors from the concentration camps. The JDC provided some cash and some food, but mostly it helped by giving people a few pieces of furniture, bedding, kitchen supplies and hand-me-down clothing. Mama inquired if they could help her obtain a sewing machine so that we could start earning some money. They said that they could, and did.

That sewing machine became our lifeline. We found a two-room apartment on the second floor at number 62, right across the street from 83 Rue François-Joseph Navez. The two rooms were fairly spacious. The first room had a white, enameled stove with a fairly large cooking surface and a big oven for baking or keeping food warm for the Sabbath. The stove also served as central heating, keeping the room warm during the cold winter months. The room had enough space for the table and four chairs that we'd also gotten from the JDC. We took some of Uncle Alex's and Aunt Lea's items out of storage, where Monsieur and Madame Petoud had put them, including the amazing convertible Murphy/bookcase bed, and put it against longest wall in the room. The Petouds also returned all the photo albums we had given them for safekeeping, as well as those belonging to Uncle Alex and Aunt Lea. They also gave Mama two silver Sabbath candelabras that had belonged to her sister.

The second room in the apartment would serve as a bedroom for the three of us. We placed a metal double bed and a single bed given to us by the JDC in that room. The JDC also gave us a small couch that fitted nicely right next to the entrance door of the apartment. The sewing machine, our prized possession, rested under the window of the large kitchen, our "multipurpose" room. The window looked out to the back of the building and was located just a few feet above the flat roof of a lower part of the building that extended toward the back. Once we were settled, we often climbed out the window and used the rooftop as a patio.

It wasn't long before Mama found work making ladies' slips. She taught me how to use the sewing machine so that I would be able to help her. Though we wanted to bring my sisters back home to Brussels, there was still more to do before we were ready to fetch the girls. In the meantime, we presented ourselves at the JDC offices every morning because they posted lists with the names of people from Belgium who had survived the concentration camps and might soon be returning home. Every time we went, we went with hope in our hearts. But we always came back dejected because we never found names on the lists that belonged to our family members. There was no way to learn the fate of our family from Romania, either. That part of Europe was still cut off from Western Europe and was under the control of the Russians.

We wanted to contact Papa in New York, but the mail service was still disorganized and international mail was not yet restored between Europe and the United States. We were also not sure of his address. The last time we had a letter from him had been in early 1940, and now it was late October 1944. Many things had happened over those four years and we had no idea where he was or if he even knew we were alive.

Once we started to earn some income from our sewing, Mama decided we were established enough to bring my sisters back to Brussels. The trains were running on a more regular schedule and buses were on the roads. It was still dangerous because there were still pockets of German resistance in several places and though the German Army in Belgium had officially capitulated, there was an unexpected major battle that developed in the region of the Ardennes early in December. This battle was quite intense and no one knew how it would end, because the Ardennes were at the opposite end of the country from Brussels.

When the time was ripe, Mama assigned me to go to the convent and bring my sisters back. I took the train from the Gare du Nord to Ghent, and from Ghent I took the train to Tielt and then finally took one more train to Ruiselede. My sisters gave me an exuberant reception and jumped all over me, but their excitement and happiness knew no bounds when they heard they would be coming back to Brussels with me. We spent the night in Mama's old room and after we had prepared ourselves to leave early the next morning, we chatted the whole night away.

The Reverend Mother refused to let us leave until I accepted a big package of food she had prepared, including a delicious loaf of fruit and bread pudding and several other items. Sisters Marie Consolata, Marie Amata, Jeanne Marie and some other nuns came to bid us farewell. They were very emotional as they said good-bye, hugging and kissing us. I never realized it, but in the thirteen months that we spent at Our Lady of Seven Sorrows, I had grown attached to the Reverend Mother and all the others who had cared for us. I promised them that we would return to visit. I also promised that we would never forget them or what they did for us.

Sister Marie Consolata walked us to the Ruiselede railroad station. Expelling thick white smoke from its locomotive stack, the train pulled noisily into the open air, single-track station and came slowly to a stop. Sister Marie Consolata's eyes filled with tears as she embraced each one of us again, then wished us a good journey while she helped us up the train steps. She did not leave the station immediately, but stayed on the platform waving to us until the train pulled away and we were out of each other's sight. I kept my promise to those wonderful sisters by writing to them often and visiting the convent every few years.

At last we were on our way home. We changed trains in Ghent for the final leg of the journey to Brussels, but the train was late. Like many other passengers we waited and waited for the train's arrival. By this time, we were exhausted from staying up all night and from the excitement of being together again. We could not believe it. We were traveling without a chaperone or guide, standing with other people who were waiting for the train and we did not have to be afraid. We no longer had to hide our identity or ourselves. It was exhilarating, but it also felt strange.

Since I had already been back in Brussels with Mama, I had gotten somewhat used to not having to hide, but Charlotte, now eleven and Betty, now eight, found it very new and disconcerting. It felt strange to them to be away from the convent. Betty asked me if she could now use her real name, but she was not completely sure what her real name was. Charlotte told her it was Mendelovits. I suggested she should wait until we were in Brussels with Mama before using it.

Why did I do that? I don't really know. Perhaps deep inside I was still not completely at ease myself.

Our train pulled into the Gare du Nord in Brussels at about two o'clock in the afternoon. We picked up our bundles, left the train station, and took the trolley to Schaerbeek. It was a short walk to the apartment house and Charlotte and Betty were bubbling with eagerness to see Mama. When we reached 62 Rue François-Joseph Navez, I asked, "Who wants to ring the doorbell?" Betty's hand flew up. I showed her which bell button to press. She pressed the button, the bell rang, and a few minutes later the door opened and Mama appeared. Both Charlotte and Betty dropped their packages and jumped up to hug Mama.

What a reunion! Mama cried as she embraced my sisters. I picked up the bundles my sisters had dropped, because they could not let go of Mama. With both children clinging to her, we headed up the stairs. What joy! The four of us were safely together again at last!

That evening, Mama prepared a special supper. After we ate, we sat and talked for a short while. Charlotte and Betty were exhausted and Mama and I were also tired, so we made it an early night. Mama wanted us to bathe first, but there was no bathroom with a bathtub. Mama pulled out the oval metal bathtub and placed it in the middle of the kitchen. She heated water on the stove, and after the tub was filled, my sisters and I took a bath that we completely enjoyed. Then we were ready for a good night's sleep in freedom, in our own place.

On the Monday after we were reunited, Mama and I escorted the girls to the elementary school on Rue Capronnier, where we enrolled them. We explained to the principal, new at the school, that the children had previously attended classes at the school but had used pseudonyms before we left Brussels to hide from the Nazis. We also explained that the children might need some extra help with the curriculum. The principal was sympathetic and seemed to understand our problem, so we left the girls at the school and told them that I'd be back for them at the end of the school day to bring them home. What a sweet word, home. After that first day, though, the girls would have to get there and back on their own.

When the paperwork was done, Mama and I went back to the apartment to work. We developed a system where we were able to produce more slips per day than we had before, and since we were paid by the piece, it helped us augment our income. Mama taught me how to hand-finish the top and bottom hems. Since lace for trimmings was exorbitantly expensive, we decorated and finished them by scalloping the bottoms and tops of each slip. I became quite skilled at doing this. We stitched the shoulder straps of the slips by machine, then turned them inside out and pressed them flat.

We also recruited my sisters. After they had come home from school, eaten their snacks and finished their homework, they joined Mama and me producing slips. Mama taught Charlotte how to machine stitch the straps, and Betty was taught to turn the straps inside out and press them. Betty was also our delivery girl. We all worked hard, but our income was still too small. Mama looked for work that would be more lucrative and I looked for an outside job. We decided that we could not stop sewing slips, but we needed to earn more.

It was early 1945, and Mama continued to go to the offices of the JDC to scan the lists and see whether she would find any family names. This soon became an exercise in futility and eventually Mama stopped hoping. We knew that, Harreke born in 1938, the youngest son of Mendel and Chany Olszyn (Uncle Alex's sister), was probably alive. While Mendel and Chany, and their teenage son, Jackie, were hiding in a clandestine apartment in Brussels, Harreke had also been hidden in a convent by Père Bruno. Mama and I planned on asking the monk where he had placed Harreke so that we could bring him home with us until his parents and brother were found.

Meanwhile, the fighting in the Ardennes had not yet subsided. V2 rockets were launched towards Antwerp and elsewhere, and the noise they made was deafening and frightening when they flew overhead. It grew worse as the rockets drew closer to their targets. Just when we were convinced that they would land on us, because of the horrible roar, they would pass us and have still more miles to go before they exploded. Sometimes, when Mama was not home and the V2's flew over, we would be terrified and huddle together with our hands over our ears to block out the racket. This especially affected Charlotte, who was unable to tolerate very loud noises. By January 1945, the Allies were able finally to turn back the German Ardennes offensive.

Once we were settled in, Mama and I visited Monsieur Ranson. He was delighted to see us. Later, we brought along Charlotte and Betty, which made him happier still. Throughout the years I would stay in touch with him, as I had with all the nuns who sheltered us. I visited him several times in Oostende and Brussels until just before he died in 1978.

Monsieur Ranson had been a courageous man during the war. We were not the only people he had hidden during those years when the Nazis pursued Jews. He had also hidden a Jewish family on the upper floor of the building across the street from his factory, in the factory offices and the employees' cafeteria.

We also often visited the Fiers and the Hottons, who deserved our heartfelt thanks for having helped us during the dangerous war years – our feelings toward these incredibly brave people was indescribable.

Mama found a job sewing linings into fur coats – the job title was fur finisher. This provided a somewhat better income, but we still struggled. I found an outside job filling boxes with powdered detergent. I was the youngest employee in the shop, which was situated above a shoe repair shop. The staircase leading down to the street floor had to be washed weekly, and that became my job as well. I thoroughly disliked what I was doing, but we needed the income. It was not long, though, before I was able to quit.

We heard that designing and making dress patterns paid well, so at Mama's suggestion, I took a pattern-making course that lasted several months and rewarded me with a diploma declaring me a skilled pattern maker. But no one offered me a job, so I decided it would be more elegant to work in an office and took a course on bookkeeping and stenography at a business school on Boulevard Adolph Max in the city center. After classes, I continued making slips at home, but when I completed the business courses, I was able to get a job as a file clerk. It didn't last long because I made a terrible mistake. I had papers to give to the office manager and didn't wait to hear his reply after I had knocked on the door. I opened the door and entered his office, only to quickly retreat mumbling, "I am sorry, I am sorry." My manager was sitting in his reclining chair, but he was not alone. One of the female staff members was sitting on his lap!

In May 1945, the war in Europe officially ended. The streets of Brussels were filled with military men – British, American, and even Palestinian Jews who had joined the British Armed Forces. There were celebrations and excitement, but our joy was tempered because so far, none of our family members had come back from the concentration camps.

CHAPTER 13

Rebuilding Our Lives

One day, as Mama sat on the trolley, a British soldier approached her and asked in a whisper, "Yiddish?" Mama nodded her head affirmatively. They spoke in Yiddish and became friends. His name was David Rosenthal and he visited us a few times and tried to help us find Papa in America, but he was transferred before he could find anything out. Then we met Willy, who was also Jewish and British, and he worked really hard to help us find out about Papa. He succeeded, but by the time we had discovered that, he'd been transferred out of Brussels, too.

In September 1945, we attended High Holy Day Rosh Hashanah services at the large Dutch Synagogue in Brussels. The sanctuary was filled with the faithful. As we sat and listened to the rabbi's sermon, there was a commotion in the back of the sanctuary. The rabbi suddenly stopped and looked over the congregants' heads toward the back. When he saw the reason for the commotion, he smiled, pointed to the back of the sanctuary and said: "We are honored to have with us a hero, an exceptional man, a man who saved many of our people from the grip of the Gestapo…Dom Bruno Reynders." Every head was now turned toward the back, the rabbi's words followed by thunderous applause.

When the applause subsided, the rabbi told us we would have a chance to greet Père Bruno after the service. Many of us headed toward the back of the sanctuary to greet him, but he was gone. He was a hero, but he was also a very modest man who was not comfortable with praise. What he had done was truly heroic. He had managed to find hiding places for about three hundred children and ninety adults, thus saving them from the murderous grip of the Gestapo. During those treacherous times, he had found places and convinced people to shelter lost souls such as us. With an accomplice, he had managed to steal blank identity cards and a municipal stamp to legalize them. He had put false names on those cards and forged all sorts of documents.

At some point during the war, an informer had led the Gestapo to understand that a monk was hiding people. As a result, Père Bruno had gone into hiding himself, but not physically. He forged six identity cards for himself, each bearing a different name, a slightly different birthplace and date, a different profession, and a different residence. But they all bore Père Bruno's photograph, though in some he wore civilian clothing, in others, clerical garb. Whichever he wore, Père Bruno continued to perform his "illegal" work to save lives.

Not long after the High Holy Days, Père Bruno came to visit us. We greeted him warmly and offered him something to eat and drink. He refused and said he was neither hungry nor thirsty at the moment. He asked me what I was up to, and I told him how I had lost my job as a file clerk, and how I was working at home with Mama, making lingerie, and that Mama wanted me to become an apprentice dressmaker. She felt that if I had skills, I would be assured of earning a livelihood, no matter where in the world I would eventually live and whether or not I knew that country's language. Such skills could tide me over until I learned the local language. Of course, Mama believed I would settle in the United States, because that is where Papa had been since 1938 – but here it was, 1945, and we still hadn't been able to contact him.

Mama was convinced that immigrating to the United States would be difficult, because she remembered how difficult it had been to get visas before the war. Papa was lucky his sister had emigrated from Romania immediately after World War I – with the help of family members who came even earlier. She was an American citizen and could help him, but would that help us now? Mama did not know. She hoped so, but was worried that the quota for Romanians was very low.

While we talked with Père Bruno, my sisters came home and were surprised to see him. They greeted him politely and shyly and he warmly returned their greetings. By then it was four o'clock, when we usually ate a light meal, known as a collation. Mama did not wait for Père Bruno to tell her whether he was hungry or not. She prepared the meal while my sisters set the table and Père Bruno continued talking to me.

He asked me if I would prefer to go to school full time. I told him, "Of course, I would like nothing better; I would love it. It would give me a chance to learn all sorts of things, but I must earn money for the family. Mama cannot make enough money to support us on her own."

He told me he would take this issue up with Mama. Then the five of us sat at the table and enjoyed our meal enormously. We had enough chairs for everyone, and took great pleasure in hosting Père Bruno. While we chatted, I thought about being able to fulfill my dream of going to a real school, full time. I also thought about my cousin Harreke Olszyn. By now he would be seven years old, and I knew Père Bruno, who was responsible for saving so many of us, had placed him somewhere in the country. So far, we had no news to indicate that his parents and brother were still alive – all three had been arrested by the Gestapo and deported. I told Père Bruno we would love to visit Harreke and bring him home to stay with us. He said he would work on it and let us know.

When we had finished eating and cleared the table, Mama directed my sisters to start working on their school assignments. Once they got busy, Père Bruno asked Mama if they could chat in private. They went into the other room, while I sat at the table with my sisters.

Mama and Père Bruno spoke quietly, but they were loud enough for me to hear part of what they said. I heard Mama say, "Absolutely not; you have done enough. Yes, I would like to be able to send her to school on a full-time basis. She loves to learn, she reads every free moment she has, but you have truly done enough. It is time for you to rest now. You have saved my children's lives. Now it is my turn to care for them from here on."

Somehow, Père Bruno convinced Mama to change her mind. The following morning, after Charlotte and Betty left for school, Mama took me to a Catholic school that was run by the Order of Notre Dame de Joie (Our Lady of Joy) in the center of Brussels. When we arrived, it looked like we were expected, and when Mama mentioned Père Bruno's name, no questions were asked. Later we found out that Père Bruno's biological sister, Sister Bernadette, was a member of that Order.

The Sister who was the headmistress told Mama that Père Bruno had already chosen my courses and had added extra-curricular typing and piano lessons. I could barely contain my surprise, happiness, and excitement. I felt like jumping for joy, but I restrained myself.

"Piano lessons for me?" I exclaimed. I could not believe it.

"Yes," she replied.

"But I have no piano on which to practice," I said, disappointment reflected in my voice.

"Don't worry. We have a piano in the parlor of our convent, just across the street. You can come there an hour or forty-five minutes before classes begin in the morning, practice, and then go to class. Follow me and I will show you where to go and where the piano is."

Mama and I followed the nun to the building across the street and walked into a spacious foyer. She opened a door to the right of the entrance, and there it was. My eyes feasted on the shiny black piano that stood there, waiting to be played.

I was enrolled on a Thursday in late September of 1945 and began my classes the following Monday. Mama was worried that I would be obliged to attend classes in catechism, but she was quickly put at ease. Père Bruno, on his own initiative, requested I be excused from attending catechism class and from participation in religious ritual. I was given study time during those periods.

I received my first piano lesson on Tuesday, right after school. The typing class met for forty-five minutes twice a week, on Mondays and Wednesdays, after school let out. I thoroughly enjoyed playing the piano and typing.

My only problem in school came from not being a native French-speaker. I knew how to speak and read French, the language spoken in Brussels, but I still had difficulty with the writing and spelling because I'd spent the last thirteen months hiding in Ruiselede, the center of the Flemish countryside. But I worked hard and soon enough mastered the spelling and grammar.

I was happy in my classes, but socially, I was very much alone. The other girls were all good friends and probably had attended school together for several years. Being the new girl at school, I knew no one, and now it was hard for me to break the ice and find friends.

Before the war I used to make friends easily and was comfortable with people. But after hiding who I was for so long, and being responsible for my sisters' lives, I had changed without realizing it. I had more difficulty relating to people my age because I felt so much older. I was also more reticent with people

I'd just met – which probably made me less approachable. My most cherished moments at the school were the ones I spent playing the piano in the convent's elegant parlor. There, sitting alone at the piano, I was totally at peace.

As time went by, our little family developed a routine. After school, I'd go home and sew some more slips for Mama, while Charlotte and Betty helped with the straps. Once Mama came home from work, we'd prepare dinner together and, after we had eaten and cleared the table, Mama would do some household chores while we did our homework. We spent our evenings together.

When it got colder and we needed coal for the stove, we tried to save money by going down to the railroad tracks, just as we had during the war, to collect coal that had fallen off the trains. Mama taught us to be resourceful and stretch our francs, and the day finally came when she was able to tell Père Bruno, who was always there to assist us, that we were finally able to manage on our own, and that we were eternally grateful to him for saving our lives.

Some time in October, on my way home from school one day, I saw a familiar face as I waited at the trolley stop. I was not sure if "he" was who I thought "he" was, because "he" was taller than I remembered. "He," however, called out, "Flora, is that you?"

I tentatively replied, using his nickname, "Dudi?"

We were surprised and happy to see each other; he was a friend from before the war. I learned that Dudi (David), now seventeen, survived by being hidden, and he and his mother were the sole survivors of their family. He asked about us and I told him Mama would be happy to know we had run into each other. I wrote down our address and he wrote down his.

It wasn't long before we began "seeing" each other, with Mama's permission of course. Needless to say, I soon fell in love.

Dudi had joined a new group of young Jewish survivors between the ages of fifteen and twenty who planned to immigrate to the Yishuv, to Mandatory Palestine – later to become the State of Israel. He urged me to join the group, and I did. We met regularly, enjoyed each other's company, and talked about our future in Israel. I felt totally at home with Dudi and the young people in our group. It was a feeling of belonging and bonding I had not felt for a long time. When we talked to each other, we did not have to explain what we meant. We knew exactly what each us of felt.

I told Mama that one day I would marry Dudi. She said Dudi and I were too young to even think of such matters and that at the moment the only thing that mattered was to prepare for a possible future in America. That future did not include Dudi, as much as she liked him, unless he would settle in America. Besides, she said, young people fall in and out of love many times before they find the one person with whom they will share their lives.

"But Mama! Is it not better for all of us to go to Israel, which has been the Jewish people's eternal home? There, we will never have to worry about people persecuting us, and we will never have to hide because we are Jewish." I argued, but I could not persuade her.

I continued to attend the young people's meetings with Dudi, hoping that by the time the group was ready to leave for Israel, Mama would change her mind and let me go. I felt strongly that my future was with Dudi and life in Israel. But it was not to be. Early in 1946, Dudi and the others left Belgium to make their way to Israel.

Many years later, when Dudi and I were married to different people with families of our own, he in Israel and I in America, we saw each other again. We had stayed in touch throughout the years, so when we visited Israel, we went to see Dudi, who lived in Netanya. Then, every time we came to Israel, we made sure to see each other. On my visit to Israel in 1998, I called Dudi's home and learned from his wife that he had recently died after suffering from a prolonged illness.

One fall day in 1945, Père Bruno told Mama that we would be able to visit Harreke. I was delighted when Mama gave me the news. Harreke was staying at the convent of the Sisters of Don Bosco, in St. Anne, Courtrai. Because Mama would not leave Charlotte and Betty alone and it was too expensive for all of us to go, I went to see him by myself. His memory of me was vague, but I was not totally unfamiliar to him. I was allowed to spend one hour with him before I had to leave. The Mother Superior told me that I would be allowed to return to visit him on Sundays.

Now I had a problem I needed to resolve. I had to choose between visiting Harreke and attending our group meetings. It was a difficult decision to make, but I decided that visiting Harreke was the imperative. I really had no choice. This child was all alone without any family. How could I disappoint him? I could see Dudi and my friends during the week, but Harreke could be visited only on Sundays, and it was my duty to do so. He had no one else. So far, his parents and brother had not been heard from.

Whenever I came to see him at the convent, Harreke was radiant with happiness. I loved looking at his happy face during our one-hour visits. I taught him some Yiddish songs that Mama had taught me as a little girl and sang them with him – "A little boy went for a walk in the woods and caught himself a little bird...." I read him fairytales from a book I would bring with me, but no matter what we did to stretch the time, the hour went by much too quickly. When it came time to part, the separation was always painful. Harreke would hold on to me, wanting to go with me. He could not understand, he said, why he was not allowed to go home with his cousin, Flora. Neither could I. With an intervention from our wonderful Père Bruno, I was finally permitted to bring Harreke to our apartment for weekend visits from Friday afternoon until Sunday evenings, when he returned to the convent.

On Fridays, I had no extra-curricular lessons so I was free to go and pick up Harreke. I was also excused before the end of classes to give me enough time to get back before Shabbat candle lighting times. The headmistress was very kind and understood my responsibility. I would take the train to Courtrai and then make my way by trolley car to St. Anne. Harreke, holding his little bundle of clothing for the weekend would be anxiously waiting for me, and as soon as he saw me his face would light up with a smile.

Harreke glowed with happiness when he was with us. He relearned his lessons about Shabbat and watched intently when Mama lit the candles on Friday evening and we said the blessings over the wine and the *challah* (braided bread). He loved playing with Charlotte and Betty.

When we would arrive back at the apartment in Schaerbeek, Mama and my sisters would welcome Harreke with hugs and kisses, which he savored. One of the things he looked forward to was to sit down next to the metal bathtub filled with water in the middle of the kitchen floor. It was not the tub that attracted him, but the fish swimming around in it.

In order to prepare for Shabbat, Mama would buy a live carp during the week – filling our metal bathtub with cold water before she went to the fishmonger. When she'd come back, she would put the carp into the bathtub, where it would swim around until Friday morning. Like Harreke, my sisters enjoyed watching and playing with the carp during the few days it lived in the tub.

But after we left for school on Friday mornings, Mama would take the carp out of the tub, smack it on the head and prepare it for our Shabbat meal.

Then she'd wash out the tub so that it would be ready for my sisters' bath after they came home from school. Mama changed her routine somewhat once Harreke started spending weekends with us. She would wait until Harreke arrived and let him play with the carp for a while before removing it from the tub – if there was enough time left to prepare it for the Sabbath. As the days became shorter, the carp would not be used for the Sabbath, but would be kept alive over the weekend so Harreke could play with it to his heart's content. Of course, while the carp occupied the tub we could not bathe, but we were able to wash ourselves with water directly from the faucet.

Taking Harreke back to the convent became an agonizing experience for both of us. He was so happy when he was with us, causing me to ask Mama repeatedly why he couldn't stay with us. If his parents returned, I would be happy to hand him over to them, but to take him back to strangers every week was extremely painful. Mama said it was against the law because he was related to us only by marriage, not by blood.

During one of my conversations with Mama I suggested, "Mama, we can hide him; after all, we were hidden and no one found us...I'll find a good hiding place for him in case the gendarmes come looking for him – he'll be safe."

"You don't understand, *Mamele* (little mother). Things are different now. The Gestapo is gone and now we must do things according to the law. Now we must obey all the laws."

I was not happy about this because Harreke had become very attached to me, the big, fifteen-year-old adult. Every Sunday, Harreke, now almost seven years old, cried and screamed, "Flora, do not leave me; please Flora, I do not want to stay here. I want to go home with you..."

Going home without Harreke was also difficult for me. I could not understand why we could not keep him, and I had incredible feelings of guilt. There must be a way ...but there was no way. At that time Jewish children who were sheltered in religious or secular institutions were, according to Belgian law, legally retained in their custody until the biological parents or families returned to claim them.

Willy, the Jewish British soldier who befriended us and tried to help us find information about Papa, visited us while he was still in Brussels. Sometimes he would join us for a Shabbat meal. Harreke and my sisters especially enjoyed his company and would vie for a spot to sit close to him at the dinner table. These evenings gave Willy a feeling of home, as he watched the flames of the Shabbat candles flicker, sharing and leading us in our prayers, and partaking of the ceremonial wine and *challah* with us. We were allowed a small sip of wine after we recited the blessing, "*Baruch Atah Hashem, Elokeynu Melech Ha Olam, Borei Pri Ha Gafen*" ("Blessed are you God, our Lord, King of the Universe, creator of the fruit of the vine.")

Occasionally, Willy would join us for an outing to the city center. He loved sightseeing in Brussels and so did we, for at last we were free to enjoy the city in which we lived. We took great pleasure in seeing it through Willy's eyes.

Then, during a visit at the Petouds, Madame remembered Uncle Alex's mandolin and the other items they were holding for safekeeping. Realizing that Uncle Alex and his family would, in all probability, never return, she insisted that Mama accept their legacy. It was a pleasant but sad visit – it was a turning point, for it was that visit that forced us to accept the fact that our family was lost.

As we walked home, my eyes scanned the Place de la Cage aux Ours, the round "square" with the little park in front of the Petoud's apartment house. I remembered our happy times with Uncle Alex, Aunt Lea and Nounou. Now, there were just the four of us, Harreke, the little cousin we could not keep, and Papa in faraway America.

CHAPTER 14

The Christmas Box

Once a child in Belgium turned fifteen years old, she or he was required to carry an identity card with their full name, address, day and year of birth, marital status, profession, and nationality. Two weeks before my fifteenth birthday, which was on August 10, 1945. I presented myself at the municipal building to register and receive an official identity card. I could not wait. This was a new phase in my life, and I thought it would make me an official adult. I was required to bring two photographs and my birth certificate. I had my birth certificate because it was among the items Mama had given to Madame Petoud for safekeeping. After I filled out several forms, one of the clerks examined my documents, took the two required photographs I'd brought with me, and told me to return in eight days to pick up my card.

Eight days later I came back, feeling like a grown-up, for I would have my own identity card. When I got there, the waiting room was full, so I found a seat and waited with anticipation. Finally, my name was called. I got up from my seat and went to the clerk. "I am Flora Mendelovits," I said as I presented myself proudly. He handed me my identity card. But something was wrong. He must have handed me the wrong card. How could he make such a mistake? I was expecting a green identity card. After all, I was a native Belgian, a very proud Belgian. The card he handed me was the card for legal foreign residents. It was not the green identity card that I, as a Belgian, expected. The card looked like Mama's. It was yellow, with a three-quarter-inch wide red band across all three pages of the card. This red band had two words printed on it in French and Flemish: *Étranger* and *Vreemdeling* (foreigner).

This could not be! Something was terribly wrong. I handed the identity card back to the clerk and exclaimed, "Somebody made a mistake; you are giving me the wrong card!"

The clerk calmly replied: "No, mademoiselle, we did not make a mistake. This is the right card." No, no, I thought. He is wrong. "Let me speak to the manager of the office, please," I continued.

The clerk left to fetch the manager, who came out of his office. By this time, I was quite agitated and presented my complaint, but he also insisted that they had given me the correct card. I took the card and opened up the folded three-page document to the side where it showed the place of birth. I pointed to where it clearly noted my birthplace: Berchem, a neighborhood in Antwerp, one of the major cities in Belgium. Yet, on the line alongside "nationality," it showed "*roumaines*," meaning Romanian. By now I was shouting.

The manager handed the card back to me and said, "Mademoiselle, take your card and go, immediately! If you do not leave right now, I will call the gendarmes." I was devastated. I was humiliated in front of all the people sitting in the waiting room. My head hung low as I left the municipal building, my legs leaden, as if saddled with heavy weights. Tears flowed down my cheeks. I could not believe what they'd said.

I was a foreigner? I was not Belgian? How could I not be Belgian? I was always such a proud Belgian. I loved the country I thought was mine. When I finally made it home, Mama explained what she already knew but had not thought about earlier – that one can only be Belgian if three prior generations, one's parents, grandparents and great-grandparents, were Belgian. Birth on Belgian soil alone did not give one the right to citizenship.

It took time for me to adjust to the fact that I was a foreigner in the country where I was born. I later learned that I was also not considered a Romanian by the Romanians because I was not born there. I was officially stateless but I had no time to dwell on this because life demanded my complete attention.

One afternoon, I came home after a visit to the Petouds, took off my coat and tried to play Uncle Alex's mandolin. I didn't have much time to practice on it and was not altogether delighted by the fact that it was now in my possession. An important part was missing. That part was Uncle Alex. I remembered how he'd sat patiently and taught me to draw beautiful sounds from its strings. I remembered how he played and how Mama sang along. Mama had a beautiful voice. Those who heard her sing said she had perfect pitch.

She would tell me stories about her life as a teenager in Romania and one of them was about her uncle in Bucharest, a singer in the opera there. When he heard Mama's voice, he asked *Zeyde* to let Mama come to Bucharest to live with him and his family, offering to teach her and train her for a possible career in opera. But this was not to be. *Zeyde* was Orthodox and followed the strict rules of his religion. These rules forbade females from appearing on the public stage, an act considered immoral.

Mama never fulfilled her dream of being a professional singer. But now, at home with my sisters and me, she sang to the accompaniment of the mandolin, though my playing was mediocre. I also got a chance to play when Harreke came "home" for the weekend. He enjoyed my playing because did not know the difference between good and bad musicianship.

Père Bruno was transferred out of Brussels, taking the little help he had extended to us went with him. Mama, unless desperate, never asked for handouts. She knew how much I loved school and my piano lessons. Reluctantly, she decided that I had to leave school and work to bring in extra funds to meet our expenses. My sisters were still too young to help very much. I left school and gave up the typing course and piano lessons I so loved. I got a job with a dressmaker, which helped to make ends meet while I learned the trade from a professional.

December 1945 started on a dismal note. The weather was cold and it was so wet from the daily rains that the wallpaper in our apartment was literally falling off the walls. We were constantly pasting the edges down. The damp days and lack of sunshine affected our moods. To make things worse, we still had no news of Papa. Mama wondered aloud if he was alive. It had been a long time – seven and a half years had passed since she had last heard from him.

Then the festival of lights, Hanukkah, was upon us. For the first time in many years we were able to light Hanukkah candles and celebrate our freedom, just as our ancestors had done thousands of years ago. They had reconsecrated the holy temple in Jerusalem and witnessed the miracle of watching a one day supply of oil burn in the *menorah* for eight days. Mama raised her crystal clear voice and sang the Hebrew prayer over the candles and we sang with her.

That evening, for a short time we were at peace. But then Mama burst into tears. We knew why. She was still waiting and wondering if she would ever see any members of our family again. She was still resisting the possibility that they were never going to return, or that they would not receive a proper burial.

School closed for the winter holidays and wouldn't reopen until January 2, 1946. Mama went to work in a fur shop every day, so I took time off from work to stay home and care for my sisters until school reopened. The dressmaker was kind and understood – she even allowed me to bring some work home. The three of us spent our vacation sewing slips, work we never totally abandoned because it brought in a little revenue.

When we had a little free time we visited the large department stores to "ooh" and "ahh" at the extravagant Christmas decorations and displays. The economy, however, had still not returned to normal. The days flew by and December 25 arrived. We were home because on this day, an official holiday, all businesses were closed. Suddenly, the doorbell rang. Mama wondered who it could possibly be, for we were certainly not expecting any visitors, and there was no mail delivery that day. She sent me down to see who it was.

When I opened the door, there was an American soldier standing there with a large package in his arms. I asked him in French, *"Puis-je vous aider, monsieur?"* (May I help you, sir?) I asked.

"Yes, I'm looking for Madame Mendelovits," he replied. Though I did not understand English, I knew that he meant Mama. So, I nodded my head in an affirmative reply. He handed me the box, which was quite heavy and, as he turned to leave, he shouted a cheerful "Merry Christmas!" I had no idea what those words meant.

I was left standing at the door with the box in my arms. When I got over my shock, I ran up the stairs with the heavy box in my arms and shouted, "Mama, Mama, an American soldier came and brought us a box."

We noticed a white envelope taped to the top but we paid no attention to it. Our curiosity to find out what was in the box propelled us into ripping it open before we did anything else.

The box was filled with food – all kinds of food – canned, jarred, bagged and boxed. There were also several bars of chocolate, my favorite. One can was marked "Spam." We opened it and saw what looked like a tasty pink loaf. It looked good and when we tasted it, it tasted good, so we ate it. We also ate other foods in the box, for we had not seen such variety in many years. Once we started eating, we could not stop and ate and ate until we could not eat anymore.

Before the war began, our family had kept to the Jewish tradition and ate only kosher foods, foods that were permitted in our religious tradition and eaten according to certain rules. During the war, we abandoned this observance, eating whatever we could find to assuage our hunger – and Jewish law allows this. Now, after the liberation, we once again attempted to observe the dietary laws, but it was difficult. Kosher food was hard to find and very expensive, even more expensive than regular food, which was already costly.

When we were done stuffing ourselves, Mama remembered the white envelope taped to the top of the big box and went to get it. It was from American Military Headquarters in Brussels, where the food must have come from. They asked that Mama present herself at their headquarters after the holidays. We were the family of an American war veteran, and were now charges of the American Army, who would take us under their wing until they could transport us to the United States and reunite us with Papa.

Apparently Papa had joined the U.S. Army during the war while we were hiding in Belgium. The American soldiers who notified officials in Belgium to put in a search for Papa must have done so. However it happened, the box of food and the official letter from the Army was our first indication that Papa was alive and well. Then things began to happen quickly as we got ready to immigrate to America.

As usual, nothing went smoothly. When the American officer handling our case learned that I was fifteen years old and had an identity card, he said that I could not travel as my father's dependent, but I needed my own travel papers. He suggested we see the officials in the re-established office of the American Consul. We went, but the news was not good. Mama and my sisters could travel to the United States as Papa's dependents. I had to obtain my own travel papers because I was a fully independent Belgian resident with an identity card. Mama begged the officer to find a way to let me travel with her and my sisters. She told him that she was afraid to leave me behind. To her, though I was fifteen, I was still a child. She asked if it would be possible to bring Harreke to the United States, too. She explained that he was alone, that his parents and brother were taken by the Nazis and never came back from the camps. When he heard that Harreke was not a blood relative, the answer was no. There was no way to bring him, even if we had official custody.

In any case, with the strict custody laws of Belgium, obtaining custody of Harreke was an insurmountable obstacle. The officer pitied Mama and told her that he would see what he could do to allow me to travel with my family. He asked her to come back to his office in two days.

When Mama went back, he had good news. The travel plans and route had been arranged and I was included. We would leave Belgium the first week of May, 1946. But first Mama had to secure certain documents. One was a confirmation from the Romanian Consul's office that Mama was the person she claimed to be and that we were her legal children. Then she had to obtain a certificate from the Brussels municipality showing that she was a legal resident and had submitted a change of address form. This certificate had to bear a photograph of all four of us, indicating our new address in Queens, New York. In addition, she had to obtain a certificate stating that at no time during the war years did she collaborate with the enemy.

But that was not all. Before we were given permission to leave, Mama had to submit an affidavit certifying that none of us would ever become charges of the United States government. In other words, we would never ask the U.S. for welfare. In addition, the affidavit had to state that underage children would be enrolled in school upon their arrival and would not be engaged in salaried work. This requirement applied only to my two sisters. Since I would be sixteen before the start of the school year in September, I was exempt. Later we learned Papa's income was not sufficient to provide his own affidavit to guarantee the full material support of four individuals. But Papa's brother-in-law, Izzy, who was married to Papa's sister, Sadie, earned a good income and took responsibility for providing the required affidavit.

Mama realized we were going to need to learn English and elected me to learn it so that we could communicate with the officials we needed to see. Mama found someone who agreed to give me a few lessons for a modest fee. I enjoyed the lessons and walked around, practicing my newly-learned vocabulary. I had some difficulty with pronunciation because of the spelling, especially sounds like "th" and "gh." The "th" sounded like a lisp when pronounced correctly and the "gh" was sometimes pronounced as the letter "f" at the end of some words and not pronounced at all at the end of others. Still, by the time we left Belgium, I had learned enough English to be able to ask for basic information – which was Mama's goal.

Mama told me that I could visit Harreke one more time before we left, but that I could not bring him home because if he would see us preparing to leave, it would be too shocking for him. He did not know we were going, and I dreaded the difficult and painful task of telling him.

Before I went to the convent, I first visited the offices of the Joint in Brussels and told the social workers that we were leaving for America and our little cousin by marriage, now eight years old, could not accompany us because of custody and immigration laws. I told them that he was in the convent of the Sisters of Don Bosco, where he had been hidden during the war. As Mama instructed, I asked if it would be possible for the JDC to take charge of him and place him in the newly established Jewish Home. I gave them my uncle and aunt's address in New York and told them that if his parents did not return, Mama and I would make a serious attempt to bring him to the United States as soon as possible.

When I was done with my errand at the JDC, I took the train to Courtrai for my last visit with Harreke. I kept going over in my mind how to tell him what was happening and how he would be left behind. How would I be able to convince this young child that I was not abandoning him? This poor little boy who had been hidden had not seen his older brother or his parents since 1942. This was the most difficult thing I was ever obliged to do.

I arrived at the convent and stood in front of the door, hesitating before ringing the bell. I was filled with fear and concern. Finally, I rang the bell and greeted the nun who opened the door. I did not have to tell her why I was there. She knew I'd come to visit Harreke. She accompanied me to the parlor where I waited until Harreke was brought to me. He entered and immediately ran into my arms, his face glowing with that wonderful smile of his. We visited for a while and then the time came for me to say goodbye and explain that I would not be coming back to visit. I placed him on my lap and held his face in my two hands. I began, trying to keep my voice steady, "Harreke, listen carefully to what I am going to say. First, let me tell you that I love you very much."

"I know, Flora, and I love you very much also."

As he spoke, he removed my hands from his face, placed his arms around my neck and head, and pressing his face tightly against mine, hugged me. I let him hold me like this for a few minutes and then said that I wanted him to look at me because what I had to say was very important.

I continued: "Harreke, I have to go on a trip. I have to go to America."

"I'll go with you ... you are taking me, right?"

I was stuck, I did not know what to say next, but I had to continue. "Harreke, I cannot take you with me, but ..." He did not let me finish. He started to cry.

"Harreke, listen to me, do not cry. Allow me to explain." He continued to cry, the tears wetting his face, but I had to finish my explanation and make him understand that I was not abandoning him, that our separation would only be temporary.

"Harreke, listen carefully. Yes, I have to leave now, but I promise you that I will send for you as soon as I'm settled in America. You know I keep my promises. I cannot take you with me now, but I promise, I promise, I will send for you."

The Sister came to fetch Harreke and take him back to the other children. I had asked to see the Mother Superior, and she entered the room before they left. I explained that my family was leaving Belgium and that someone from the Jewish Community would contact Père Bruno to arrange Harreke's transfer to their custody, until such time, that his parents return – if they survived the brutal concentration and slave labor camps.

I had to leave him. She nodded. She understood. Harreke pulled his hand away from the Sister and ran over to me. He threw his arms around me, and holding me tight started to cry again and to scream. "Do not go, Flora, do not leave me here! Please Flora, please, do not go. I do not want to stay here."

"Harreke, I love you, I will send for you, I promise." He took hold of my jacket lapels and did not let go. I repeated my promise several times. Harreke did not stop screaming. I embraced him and kissed him on his forehead and on his cheeks. I kissed his hands and tried to pry them loose from my lapels. Finally, the Mother Superior loosened his grip on my jacket lapels. He started to follow me. The Mother Superior threw her arms around his waist and held him. He kicked his legs trying to loosen her grip and flung his arms around, but she held on tightly. I threw him a few more kisses, promised again that I would send for him and left with his screams ringing in my ears.

Once outside, my own tears started to flow. It was so painful to leave this child. I was filled with pain and guilt. By now it was dusk. I headed for the railroad station for the train back to Brussels. By the time I got home it was dark. Mama knew as soon as she looked at me that my visit with Harreke had been difficult. She consoled me and also herself. She wished that it were possible to take him with us to America. She had tried, but did not succeed.

Laws are unfair, I thought. They are made for good reasons, I said to Mama, but then they become so inflexible. We talked about this and then Mama brought up another reason we could not take Harreke. She was confident, she said, that Mendel and Chany, as well as Jackie would be returning from the camps eventually, as would everyone else. If they did not find Harreke upon their return, they would be devastated.

Mama was a superb actress and fulfilled her role as an optimist very well. She reassured me that if Harreke's parents and brother did not return, she would find a way to bring him to live with us once we were settled in America. Knowing this helped calm me, but I could not stop thinking about that little boy and that last goodbye. That image of Harreke as I left him behind continued to haunt me.

CHAPTER 15

The Voyage to America

As soon as we were certain we were leaving, Mama gave away most of the pieces of furniture and household items to different friends and neighbors, but they had to wait to pick them up until after our departure. We still needed things in the apartment until the day we left. Our landlady kindly agreed to allow everyone in to take what we had promised them. We even gave her a list of names and the items each person was taking.

Mama managed to scrape a few francs into savings from our meager income, an admirable accomplishment. To add to our kitty, she sold the Murphy bed instead of giving it away, for she did not want to arrive in America empty-handed. She wanted to bring Papa a gift.

A gift for Papa? I couldn't believe it. I did not think that Papa deserved a gift. Should Mama deprive herself and us of needed items to purchase a gift for him – the man who had abandoned us? But buy a gift she did – a gold ring with a small rectangle of diamond chips on top. And she worked right up to the last days before our departure in order to pay for it.

During the war, I did not realize how much anger I had harbored against Papa whenever I watched Mama's sadness and frustration at being alone to care for three children. As a youngster, I could not understand why he was so far away instead of being with us. I also could not understand why had he left us by ourselves. I felt he could have waited until we could all go to America together. I was totally unaware of the obstacles in place to prevent immigration into the United States.

We found two used suitcases and packed them with our few pieces of clothing and a few possessions from which we could not part. These included the photo albums filled with the pictures of family members and friends who were taken away by the Nazis. We packed Lea's *Sabbath* candlesticks, a few books – including my instruction manual on how to make clothing patterns – and my stenography manual. Mama also packed small possessions acquired by my sisters. I also carefully wrapped Uncle Alex's precious mandolin in a pillowcase before placing it in its case so it would be safe during our voyage. Then everything was ready for our departure.

Before we left Brussels, we said our last good-byes to the Petoud and Fiers families, those cherished, kind people. Monsieur and Madame Fiers, who saved our lives by lending us their name, still lived in the same apartment at number 83. As a farewell gift, Madame Fiers presented me with her deceased son's wooden box of art supplies. We also said good-bye to that wonderful, courageous man, George Ranson.

During that visit, I learned that the Ranson factory had offices and storerooms across the street. When Mama asked what had happened to the Jewish family hidden there. Monsieur Ranson said they were fine and were now living in an apartment in Brussels. I was really surprised because I thought that we were the only Jews he had hidden during those treacherous years.

This good-bye was difficult. Monsieur Ranson had tears in his eyes and tried to wipe them away, but they kept flowing. He insisted we write to him to let him know how life was treating us in America and he hugged each of us in turn. At last we finally parted, as Mama thanked Monsieur Ranson again and again for having saved our lives while risking the loss of his own. He hugged each one of us again and, in a voice trembling with emotion, he expressed the happiness he felt for playing a "small" part in saving our lives and bringing us to this moment of joy. We promised again that we would write and come back to visit him.

We could not say good-bye to Père Bruno because he was not in Brussels, so I planned to write him from America.

The night before we left, all four of us spent a restless night. We were afraid we wouldn't wake up in time to catch the 8 o'clock train to Paris, the first stop on our journey. In Paris, we were supposed to meet with the newly-arrived American Consul to resolve the issue of my being able to travel on my mother's documents. The officials in Brussels, who said I was no longer considered a dependent, hoped that Mama would be able to obtain permission in Paris to let me travel with the family.

Once in Paris, the Consul told us that if the American Military would write up orders giving me permission to continue my journey with my family, he would give us the letter we needed. He gave us passes to travel to Le Havre, France, where we stayed at the American military camp there for a few days. Though Mama had a letter from the Consul stating I had permission to enter the United States, only the authorities in Le Havre had the discretion to decide if I would be allowed to board the *Santa Paula*, a steamship scheduled to leave a week later.

The Le Havre camp was not the most physically comfortable we'd ever been in, but it was pleasant. Still, Mama and I spent lots of time worrying about whether I would be able to travel with her. We tried to think of what we would do if I was forced to stay behind. I told Mama that I was not a baby and I could take care of myself until she would be able to send for me. She insisted she would not leave me behind.

In the meantime, the officials told us they were in touch with their superiors and were trying to get permission to allow me to board the ship on schedule. I was angry. With us in the camp were many young women who'd married American soldiers while they were on overseas duty in Europe and were waiting to be sent to the United States to join their new spouses courtesy of the American government. They were called war brides. Why could I not qualify for this courtesy as the child of an American service man? Wasn't the biological relationship to my father more important than a marriage certificate?

The day before the Santa Paula was scheduled to leave for the port of New York, Mama and I were very nervous. The Americans still hadn't told us a thing and I didn't sleep well because I had nightmares about being abandoned in France. I was brave when I spoke to Mama about taking care of myself, but the truth was just the opposite. I was frightened. What would I do? Where would I go?

Then Mama was given a hand-delivered note asking her to see the commanding officer. When she went to see him, he had good news and bad news for her. He would allow me to board the ship, but could not guarantee my entry into the country. There was a possibility I would be detained as an illegal immigrant and sent back to Europe, but he had made a unilateral decision to allow me to board the ship, because he took pity on us.

The next day we boarded the Grace Line's *S. S. Santa Paula* – sister ship to the *Santa Rosa*, *Santa Elena* and *Santa Lucia*, all ships pressed into service by the U. S. Army – with a group of war brides and military men headed home. We were thrilled that we were finally going to America to meet our Papa. What would it be like? Would we recognize him? It had been more than eight years, and Charlotte and Betty had been very young back then. I had a vague memory of him, but mostly I remembered the outings we took together. I used to sit on the back of his bicycle, holding on to his waist as we rode through the streets of Antwerp and the Stadtpark. I remember how he showed me the tools of the carpentry trade in his furniture atelier, and how I loved watching him and his employees work.

But now I was also angry. I was a child who had seen her mother struggle, crying in frustration, grief and fear, exhausted from being alone at thirty-two with three young children in the middle of a war that deliberately targeted us for extermination. He knew that. How could he leave us defenseless before the onslaught of the Nazis and Jew haters?

I did not realize that if there had not been a war with Germany, Papa would most likely have stayed in Belgium with us. What also troubled me was that Mama, teary-eyed, kept asking questions to which I had no answers. It had been a full year since the war was officially over. Did any of the family members in Belgium and in Romania survive the war? If they did, where were they?

As the ship plied the Atlantic Ocean on its way to the land of freedom, we would stand on deck and look out at the sea, fascinated by the vast expanse of water on which we were gliding. We were treated with great kindness by the ship's staff, all military personnel. Meals were served cafeteria style, and we'd sit at tables that reminded me of the refectories in the convents where we had been hidden – long tables flanked by benches on either side. The food was not elegant, but it was wholesome and satisfying and when we weren't seasick, we enjoyed it.

Until we clarified our status, everyone on the ship assumed I was a war bride who was joining my husband in the States, and that my mother and sisters escorted me as his guests. When I corrected them and proudly said that I was not a war bride, but my mother was married to an American veteran and that we were joining Papa in New York, they were even more surprised. How and why would an American military man marry a woman with three children? Mama would explain to her wondering audience that she and Papa had been married for many years, that we were Papa's children, and that he had enlisted in the American army as a volunteer.

On the third day at sea, the ocean became rough and the ship heaved up and down. I felt waves of nausea washing over me, and so did Mama and my sisters. By the fourth day we all succumbed to seasickness and our only concern was trying to keep the contents of our stomachs from making a violent exit. Then, after a few days, the sea calmed down and we felt better.

We went back out on deck during the improved weather to watch the waves and the occasional birds flying by. Sometimes we were allowed to visit the navigator's station on the bridge, where we were fascinated to learn how the helmsman steered the ship. We wondered how he knew which direction to take in the vast expanse of water and sky that had no landmarks. He showed us the compass and the other instruments that were used to chart our trip.

Our sea voyage took eight days, and when the *Santa Paula* approached the New York harbor, the sun had already set. Because it was dark, the *Santa Paula* was not permitted to pull into the dock and so had to anchor at the mouth of the Hudson River.

That night, Mama and the three of us stood on the deck, holding on to the railing and looking wide-eyed at the skyline of New York City in total disbelief. We had arrived at last in the great United States. In the distance, tall skyscrapers rose high in the sky as if they were growing out of the water, illuminated by thousands of lights. We also saw something else rising from the harbor – an island from which rose a tall, beautiful statue of a woman wearing a crown. We wondered out loud who she was, and a soldier standing nearby explained that she was the Statue of Liberty, who represented the open arms of the United States of America, a nation that received people who were oppressed in other countries and were searching for the freedom she offered. We could not tear ourselves away from the view – not believing that we had actually arrived – so we spent the entire night on deck staring at New York's skyline and the Statue of Liberty.

The thoughts in my head were scary. What would happen to me if Mama and my sisters were allowed to disembark and I was sent back to Europe? We were so close to the end of the journey, after eight years of hoping and wishing for a reunion with Papa, that it would be horrible if they sent me away. I tried to shake this thought, but could not. I said nothing to Mama. As I looked into the distance at New York, so close and yet so far away, I saw Harreke's face appear before me, wearing an accusing look. He seemed to say to me, silently, "Is it not terribly sad to be alone, without family?"

"Yes," I nodded to myself, as Harreke's face disappeared.

Guilt washed over me. This was the first time since we had boarded the *Santa Paula* that I'd even thought of Harreke. I had been so preoccupied with myself that my thoughts seemed to have excluded everyone else. How selfish of me! Now, thinking of Harreke, I wondered if his family might have returned from the camps since we left Brussels. Perhaps Harreke's parents...his brother...Aunt Lea? Before leaving, Mama left our aunt's address in New York with the Mother Superior at the convent and at the JDC, and I wondered if any letters with good news had arrived during the trip. I figured Papa would tell us if there had been any contacts. When I shared my fears of abandonment with Mama, because I needed her support, she assured me that she would not permit anyone to send me back to the old country.

On May 29, 1946, the sun rose in all its glory and lit up the skyline, brightening everything around us. We returned to our cabin to wash up and then ate breakfast in the dining room, but we weren't very hungry – we were too nervous to eat, because we had no idea what would happen next.

An announcement from one of the officers instructed everyone to return to their cabins to prepare to disembark. When the luggage was ready, we were asked to assemble on deck, where we would present our documents for final scrutiny. We went back to the cabin and, as I brushed my hair, I saw that Mama was taking a little more time than usual in front of the mirror and putting on some lipstick. Mama was always well-groomed even during the worst of times, for her philosophy, which she taught her daughters, was that no matter how besieged with problems we were, looking ill-groomed and morose would not solve them. We were taught to face the world with a smile, no matter what...for if you do, the world will smile at you, and if you cry, you will cry alone.

Charlotte, Betty and I washed our hands and faces again, re-combed our hair, and straightened our clothes. We were finally ready for whatever fate had in store for us. We took one last look around the cabin, closed the door and headed to the upper deck. Fear gripped me again as I climbed the stairs. What would I do if I couldn't get off the ship?

Other passengers had already begun gathering. There were three long lines in front of a long narrow table where the officials all sat. Two lines were for the women, and the other was for returning soldiers. Everyone waited, papers in hand, to get their landing passes stamped. When it was our turn, Mama handed our documents across the table to the military officer. He looked at the papers and looked at us, then looked at the papers again and then looked at me. We stood still. The immigration official seated next to the military officer took the papers, looked at us, then took another look at me.

My heart was beating wildly. He said nothing, just looked at me for what seemed an eternity. "Who is the bride?" he asked, and Mama pointed to herself.

Using the few words of English I knew, I pointed at Mama and said, "Soldier her husband." Then, pointing to my sisters, I continued: "Soldier her father and her father." As he had still not removed his gaze from me, I quickly added: "Oh, soldier my father also."

The two officials conversed in hushed tones. I was worried and tense, and when I looked at Mama I saw that her face also reflected her worry. As we waited for a reply, there was a commotion from the third line, where one of the war bride's papers didn't quite seem to be in order, and she was screaming at the officers at the top of her voice, in English. She slowed down the processing and people were becoming tired and irritable from standing and waiting, but the four of us stood in front of that table, not saying a word.

Finally, the military officer motioned to the immigration official, handed Mama her documents and a landing card, and waved us on, allowing us all to leave the ship together.

I did not have time to heave a sigh of relief – we turned and went toward the exit, waving our pink landing card at the guard standing at the gangplank to the dock. Another soldier helped us put our feet on American soil (actually concrete) at last, and we walked into a large waiting room filled with people who came to greet their brides, husbands and families.

Two men were walking toward us, wildly waving their arms, and as the distance between us shortened, they threw their arms open wide. One man looked vaguely familiar and the other was a total stranger. I realized that I barely recognized Papa, but something was wrong – he was so short, barely five foot six inches tall, and he had a paunch!

I did not like that. The other man, who was much taller, was Isadore, the uncle we'd never met before. Uncle Izzy was married to Sadie, my father's sister, and we'd never met her either because she had left Romania as an eleven-year-old, when Papa was a young child.

I felt strange and uncomfortable, and realized that eight-and-a-half years is a very long time in a child's life. When Papa left us in Brussels, I was a mere eight years old. Now, in New York, I was a young woman, just two months shy of sixteen.

Both men embraced us all, and Papa hugged and kissed Mama. But though I knew the man kissing her was Papa, I now found it hard to call this stranger by that title. The three of us began to refer to him as "the man" or "that man." We stood shyly by while the adults exchanged a few words before picking up our few pieces of luggage and heading toward an elegant and big, black shiny car that made my eyes widen in wonder. It was a Cadillac, and it belonged to Uncle Izzy.

"The man" opened the trunk, placed our luggage inside and slammed the trunk lid shut. Then he helped us into the car's back seat. As my sisters and I sank into this very comfortable vehicle, I could not remember ever being in such wonderfully soft and luxurious seats. I savored every moment of this luxury as my uncle drove us to our destination. Mama and "that man" sat alongside him in the front.

As we crossed New York City to get to Queens, a borough on the other side of the East River from Manhattan, my eyes swallowed whole the awesome sights of New York. The streets were filled with traffic – there were cars of every size, shape and color, trucks, motorcycles, and bicycles. The sidewalks were packed with pedestrians. Even the European cities I had visited, including Brussels and Antwerp, did not have such heavy traffic and so many people in the streets. The height and shape of the skyscrapers was mesmerizing. I had heard of them, but never imagined how huge and tall they actually were.

But what struck me and disappointed me was the garbage and litter that was strewn everywhere, something I had already noticed when we walked from the dock to the car. I was also surprised by the graffiti, all kinds of drawn images, ugly faces and signs, words I did not understand, scrawled on buildings and walls. I had dreamed of our arrival, but in my dreams I never saw dirt. I never saw garbage on the streets. I'd never seen graffiti before.

We traveled over a very large bridge, which I realize now must have been the Fifty-Ninth Street Bridge, and drove into an area that was very different from Manhattan. Here the landscape was greener and calmer, with less traffic and no skyscrapers. The buildings seemed to me to be of a more normal size. We eventually turned into a street lined with stately brick family homes surrounded by beautiful plants and trees. Uncle Izzy parked the Cadillac in the driveway of one of them and announced in Yiddish that we had arrived. *"Mir zeinen du."*

Aunt Sadie must have heard the car in the driveway, because by the time we climbed out of the car, she had come out of the house to greet us. We hauled the luggage into the house, where we met our two cousins, Harriet and Rhoda. They were somewhat younger than I was, but since I hardly knew any English, I couldn't say much. Charlotte and Betty knew no English at all, so we just looked at each other and smiled. I spoke to "that man," Uncle Izzy and Aunt Sadie in Yiddish.

We weren't in the house very long when we were seated at a dinner table laden with delicious American food. The conversation was carried on by "the man," Uncle Izzy and Mama, because Aunt Sadie was too busy running back and forth to the kitchen from the table.

The four of us were exhausted and could not even offer to help her. Even Mama, usually talkative, was quiet. The eight-year-long wait for a real home was finally over, and we were too tired even to talk. The three of us were assigned a bedroom that we thought we were going to share with Mama, so we were surprised to learn she would spend the night just across the hall. We all said goodnight to each other. Mama and "the man," came upstairs with us and came into our room. Both kissed us goodnight and left. I was not surprised when I saw him enter the room across the hall through the open door, but when Mama followed him in and closed the door behind her, I was shocked.

How would Mama prepare for bed with a man in the room? I thought she would talk to him for a while and come back to us, but she didn't. We tried to stay awake and wait for her, but we finally fell asleep.

CHAPTER 16

The American Dream

Breakfast the next morning was absolutely delicious. Then, Uncle Izzy packed us back into the car and drove us to 132 Columbia Street on Manhattan's Lower East Side, a very poor neighborhood that would become our home for the next two years. The car pulled up in front of an ugly building and stopped.

"Everybody out," shouted Uncle Izzy cheerfully. "We have arrived at your new home." Reluctantly, we all got out of the car and the luggage was unloaded. We all took our bundles, following Mama and "the man" up four flights of stairs while Uncle Izzy drove away to go on about his business. There was no elevator in this old, dark and horrible building.

As our parents preceded us into the apartment, my sisters and I looked at each other and grimaced when we took in our new abode. We put our bundles down on the floor and inspected the place. It was an ugly railroad flat – you had to walk through one room after another to get from one end of the apartment to the other.

One entered the apartment through the kitchen. There was an icebox on the left, and then the kitchen sink, flanked by a countertop on the right. Several white cabinets were hung on the wall over the sink and the countertop. Beyond the icebox, a window gave us a glimpse of the city's landscape through a metal structure that I later learned was a fire escape. (That fire escape would serve me well as a place to sleep during the intense, hot New York summer.)

151

A table and four chairs stood in the center of the kitchen. There were two more rooms to the right. One was a windowless room, furnished to serve as a dining room – with another table and six chairs, a cabinet, and a small convertible couch that became my bed. The next room had two windows facing the street and was designated to be the living room and our parents' bedroom. The room to the left of the kitchen was for my two sisters, and was also the indoor utility room, where we could hang clothes to dry and store big items.

I didn't notice until I needed one, that there was no toilet. I walked through the entire apartment, but could not find one. Puzzled, I turned to my father and asked him where the toilet was. He told me it was in the hallway, opened the apartment door and pointed to a toilet that served four families, including us, and handed me a key. I had no choice but to use it.

When we wanted to prepare for bed, we looked for a bathtub or shower and found the four-legged tub under the removable kitchen counter used to prepare meals. It had hot and cold water faucets – a small luxury we appreciated.

The icebox and some of the cabinets had been stocked with dishes, utensils, and food before we'd arrived. It was obvious that "the man" had tried to make our new home comfortable, and if we hadn't gone to Uncle Izzy and Aunt Sadie's house first, I might have been content. But the contrast between the two neighborhoods, their lovely tree-lined street and the ugly, dirty street with its garbage cans where we lived was so deep, it made me bitter. This was not the America I had dreamed of. I told Mama I wanted to go back to Belgium, and my sisters agreed with me. We hated it; it was ugly.

Mama consoled us: "Do not worry children. We will not be here for long. I will get you out of here. I promise." My father heard Mama make her promise in the singular "I." He also noticed that we did not call him Papa or Father. He heard us call him "the man," and realized we were referring to him. He also noticed how shocked and disappointed we were in this dismal place he wanted us to call home.

During breakfast the next day, our father told us he noticed that we refused to call him Papa or Father. He told us how much he loved us and how happy he was that we were all together again. He implored us to call him Papa again, the way we did when we were little and all together in Antwerp. But eight and a half years had gone by. It was extremely awkward and difficult and I resented him for having left us behind. To keep the peace, I began to call him Papa again, and after a while it became normal and I no longer thought about it.

A few days later, we had a family meeting where it was decided Charlotte and Betty would be registered at the local public school and Mama and I would look for jobs. Honorable discharge from the U. S. Army in hand, Papa could return to work. If the three of us brought home paychecks each week, and if we were frugal, we would be able to move to a nicer neighborhood.

We went to the district known as the garment center in midtown Manhattan, where the clothing industry was centered around Broadway beginning in the 1930's. Mama and I got jobs working for a dress factory doing piecework, a very high pressure job, but the more pieces we finished, the more money we made. I was very proud of myself when I handed my parents my first paycheck. All of us took a portion of our earnings and put it away to save for a better place to live, and I was given an allowance for carfare and pocket money.

I had Uncle Alex's cherished mandolin with me but its neck had broken. I still missed the violin I'd left behind in Antwerp when we escaped to hide in Brussels. I decided to save part of my allowance for the purchase of a new violin. It took me about eight months and I found a violin I could afford at a pawnshop. What excitement! What happiness! I was in America and I had a violin. I no longer noticed the ugliness of my surroundings. My world seemed suddenly beautiful again – though money was still a problem.

Mama found out that fur finishers make more money than dressmakers, and assumed that it would be the same kind of fur finishing she had done in Europe, sewing linings into fur garments. She applied for a job but the work was different, and after a few days she was fired. Always optimistic in the face of adversity, she managed to learn a few things, and found another job that lasted several weeks. She was fired again, but each time she changed jobs she learned a few more things about American fur finishing. With the same strong spirit that had helped her and us to survive during the war, she continued to work and learn.

It took some time, but eventually Mama became an expert fur finisher. Another very valuable lesson she learned was that if she joined the Fur Workers' Union, she would earn a larger paycheck. She sought out the union office and applied for membership. The officers who ran the union were sympathetic, but she would have to fulfill certain obligations before membership could be granted. One of those was to picket non-union factories for a certain number days and, if she did, they would grant her union membership with all the benefits it offered. Mama did not understand what picketing meant. They explained that she would have to walk back and forth in front of a building housing a non-union factory, carrying a sign to discourage people from either patronizing or working there.

When she came home, Papa, Mama and I held a meeting after dinner. We decided that since Mama earned more than I did, I should take time off from my job to picket. I did, and that's how Mama became a member of the Fur Workers' Union and worked in a union job in a union shop where her earnings were substantially higher. I was fired.

I found a job in a factory that made ladies' tailored jackets. It was in a cellar and was reached via a few stone steps leading down from the street. The shop windows were below street level, too, and the shop was dim and gloomy, even with the electric lights that lit up our work areas. There were six sewing machines, a cutting table and two ironing boards. A narrow table stood against one wall and held boxes containing thread, buttons, trim, and other decorations. Fabrics in a variety of colors were also stacked on the table. Nine of us worked there.

I was hired without hesitation because as someone trained in Europe, I knew how to use a sewing machine, and was also able to hand-finish a garment. My employer also liked the fact that I was familiar with pattern making. The people in this shop, including him, were friendly and kind, and it turned out to be a pleasant working experience, despite the bleak surroundings. I became something of a shop "pet" because, at sixteen, I was much younger than the others. The women I worked with often brought me things to eat!

After working there for a few weeks, I mentioned that Papa was a furniture maker and carpenter. The boss asked me to arrange a meeting because he needed someone who knew how to renovate spaces, and Papa might want to work with him. When Papa came to see him, he saw our physical working conditions, but not the pleasant working atmosphere. He was angry with my employer, a gentle man, and chastised him for allowing a sixteen year old to work under such conditions. Then Papa grabbed me by the hand and dragged me out of the shop, ignoring my protests and never even talked to my employer about the work he could have done for him.

Instead of looking for another job, I enrolled in the High School of Fashion Industries, where I improved my pattern-making skills and studied clothing design. I studied English writing, and obtained most of my English skills by going to the public library near my home and reading whenever I had a free moment. The librarian was a kind lady, who, when I asked, gave me a list of recommended books that was several pages long. I was not discouraged by the length of the list and read each book with a dictionary at my side. Whenever I finished a book, I checked it off my list. Many years later, I realized that her list consisted of classic literature and less famous but excellent works.

I quit the school, against the advice of the principal, because I had problems relating to the other students – not my lessons. My classmates seemed childish to me, and I seemed too old for them. They also mocked my European accent. After two particularly bad days when students had made insulting faces at me behind the teacher's back and then openly laughed at me when I opened my mouth to answer a question – the teacher sitting there and smiling at their insults – I yelled at them all, "You are so mean. So, I speak like a foreigner, but I speak French better than you do, and I speak Flemish, and I speak Yiddish, and all you people can only speak one language." I ran out of the room and collapsed in tears outside the classroom door, waiting for the bell to end the class.

The teacher called me in to "talk" once the students emptied the room, and acted like she was consoling me, but she never apologized for encouraging the students to make fun of me. She did admit that the students were out of order. But I said it no longer mattered because I had had enough and was quitting and would never be back. She urged me to stay and impressed upon me the importance of continuing my course work, but there was no way I would subject myself to the kind of behavior these students displayed. They were not much better than the antisemites in my classes in Antwerp and Brussels at the beginning of the war, and I would not tolerate that at all. I had lasted two semesters and had breezed through courses in English, world history, applied textiles, trade dressmaking and related arts.

By this time, Mama was especially anxious about leaving Manhattan and moving to Queens. Whenever we visited Aunt Sadie, the urge to move became stronger. My quitting school didn't bother my parents either, who encouraged me to go back to work so we could move sooner. And so, after the fiasco with the teacher and my fellow students, I went to the principal and told him I was leaving.

He insisted that one of my parents come to school to see him, so Mama came to school with me. Though he promised me a scholarship to the Fashion Institute of Technology, the famous college for clothing designers and manufacturers, Mama said the family needed the additional income I would generate.

When we were done, I went back to work in the garment district, and soon realized that working in the office – doing white collar work – was more prestigious than being a craftsman in the trade. To improve the clerical skills I had learned at the convents and at the business school in Brussels, I took an evening course at the Eron Preparatory School, a private business school, where I learned English stenography and bookkeeping, and earned a certificate that I was confident would help me find a white collar job. (It seemed that Americans thought a white collar job in an office, instead of what they called a blue collar job in the factory, implied that a person had more intelligence. The fact that the skills needed in the factory were much more complex didn't mean much. It was all a question of status and appearances. Substance, it seemed, meant nothing much to Americans.)

With my new certification as a stenographer/bookkeeper, I applied for a white collar position as a secretary/receptionist in a law firm. I got the job. For the first week, I answered the telephone, welcomed clients, and filed papers. During my second week at work, one of the attorneys called me into his office and gave me dictation, which I took down using stenography. When he was done, I typed up the letter with an envelope and knocked on his door so that I could give it to him to sign. But since he wasn't in, I placed the letter on his desk so he could see it and sign it when he came back. Then, I went back to my other duties.

When he came back to the office, he called me in and began, "Miss Mendelowitz, you are a wonderful young lady, but I am afraid I will have to let you go."

I was shocked. Before I had time to recover from my shock, he continued, "After you master the English language, come back to see me and I will gladly rehire you. You are a lovely and hardworking young woman. I am sorry."

"What did I do wrong?" I asked.

He gave me a sad look and showed me a word, an important word in the world of law that I had misspelled. I had written the word according to what I heard, *Sabena*, and it should have been "subpoena." Sabena was the name of the Belgian airline. I had never heard the word subpoena before, so that even if my English had been impeccable, the word subpoena would probably not have been in my vocabulary, because it was not a word commonly used outside of the legal profession. I began looking for another office job, convinced that blue collar jobs were beneath me. While I was looking, I spent every free moment I had at the local public library. The more I read, the better my English became, but I could not rid myself of my accent.

CHAPTER 17

Coming Into My Own

When I was young, everyone said I was stubborn. As I grew older and became a young adult, the word "stubborn" was changed to "persevering." I liked that word much better, for it had a positive connotation. I kept looking for a good job and was told there was a bilingual position available at a major textile firm, M. Lowenstein and Sons, in downtown Manhattan, near Wall Street. I applied for the job and was hired after a brief interview. There was just one bad moment. They asked if I had graduated from high school and I lied. I said yes and thankfully they didn't ask to see my diploma. I did not like having to lie, but I needed the job and I was jubilant when I got it, but also nervous. Was I good enough? Was I skilled enough? I decided that the only thing that could happen to me if my work was not satisfactory was getting fired. I started work at M. Lowenstein & Sons in the early part of 1948, and I loved working there.

The first item I asked for when I began working was a French/English dictionary. It surprised me that a large company with so many international clients did not have one, but I could not shake the feeling of insecurity relating to my knowledge of English, and it would help me tremendously. My work consisted of taking dictation in English and translating the letters into French before I gave them to my manager to be signed. Once he signed them, I sent them to the mailroom, where they were stamped and mailed. I also translated incoming mail from French to English before placing it on my manager's desk.

Whenever I did not feel totally comfortable and was not sure if the work

I had done was accurate, I would secretly take the work home and, until late in the evening, would work with the dictionary until I felt my translation was satisfactory. I would bring the finished work back to the office the following morning and place it on my manager's desk.

I commuted to work every day by subway and then walked a few blocks to the office. While I sat or stood, and the train rushed through the tunnels under the streets, my thoughts would turn to Europe, and I would remember the many members of our family who had been arrested in Belgium and were taken away by the Nazis.

Mama and I continued our search for information, to see if any of them or members of the family from Romania had survived the concentration camps. Unfortunately, most of them had not. For the rest of her life Mama often cried and mourned the loss of her father, her sisters, her aunts and uncles, and her cousins.

I was preoccupied by the memory of Harreke, whom I'd abandoned at the convent in Belgium. I could not forget him. The JDC in Brussels had taken temporary custody of him and placed him in an orphans' home for Jewish children. For a short while I wrote to them, but the letters were returned, marked "Return to Sender."

I even returned to Belgium in a futile attempt to find him and came back with a deep sadness. I had lost Harreke forever. The scene at the convent, when I had said good-bye and Harreke had begged me not to abandon him, now haunted me constantly.

In the summer of 1948, we finally moved into our own home, a spacious townhouse on Main Street in Flushing, Queens. Mama had learned that in America you can get a mortgage and make monthly payments. As a veteran, Papa applied for and got a thirty-year mortgage at a fair interest rate.

Charlotte and Betty continued their education at the public school in our new neighborhood, and I continued working at M. Lowenstein. My commute to work now took over an hour, and I had to take a bus to the subway station and then change trains before I got to downtown Manhattan, but I didn't mind because I loved working there.

I was happy. I worked hard and, as time passed, became more proficient in English and French, making my work easier. The people I worked with were friendly, and the atmosphere in the office was pleasant. No one mocked my accent as they had in other places.

Because there was a great demand for renovations and remodeling in the post-war boom, Papa, with Mama's encouragement and help, opened a remodeling/contracting firm. Mama was his business partner, bookkeeper and sales person. They both worked hard and the company flourished. Soon they were able to hire two workers. Life was good.

In 1948, while we were still living in Manhattan, I met a young fellow by the name of Jackie Singer, who was in the army. We fell in love. Both sets of parents gave us their blessing, though they felt we were too young to tie the knot.

We were married in November of 1949 at a ceremony and reception attended by some friends, co-workers and relatives who shared our happiness. When the party was over, we went to my parents' house in Queens, and a few days later, Jackie went back to his posting at Fort Jay on Governor's Island, right off the southern tip of Manhattan. I lived at home and went back to work at M. Lowenstein. A few months later, Jackie got his honorable discharge.

My parents' house had balconies on the front and back and an unfinished basement at street level with an entry door. Once Jackie was mustered out, he got a job at E.J. Korvette, then a large department store on Forty-Second Street in Manhattan. In his free time, he and Papa built us a beautiful, compact apartment with everything we could possibly need. The back door opened onto a small garden, and Jackie, with Papa's permission, put in a small pond stocked with small fish and a few frogs. The balcony from my parents' apartment above acted as an awning, providing a patch of shade and some protection from the weather if we decided to dine outdoors and enjoy the garden.

In the summer of 1951, Jackie and I learned that if all went well, we would have a baby in the wintertime. My parents were thrilled with the idea of becoming grandparents, and looked forward to the event with a great deal of excitement. Charlotte and Betty loved the idea of being aunts. Jackie and I were very, very happy – and began looking for a larger place to live.

We found a one-bedroom apartment in Jamaica, a nearby neighborhood, that had all the amenities we needed – a large living room with a big window that allowed lots of sunlight in; a full kitchen with the added luxury of a washing machine; a dining area; a full bathroom, and a nice-sized bedroom, where we set up our little nursery before the baby was born.

I found it hard to leave M. Lowenstein and Sons, but the time had come for me reluctantly to submit my resignation. I wanted my baby to have a full-time mother to care for him. Jackie was making a good living, and his company was growing.

Everyone was elated when our beautiful baby boy, Mark, made his appearance in February 1952. Our delightful daughter, Sandra (Sandy), was born in December 1954, and we had created our perfect little family. Jackie's salary grew along with the company's fortunes, and that allowed me to be a full-time homemaker and mother. It didn't take long before Jackie was able to buy our first car, a Chevrolet, which allowed us to explore the city and surrounding areas.

In 1957, Jackie was transferred to Pennsylvania, where the company was establishing a large discount department store in Springfield. We moved to Broomall, just outside Philadelphia, only three miles from his work, and our little family thrived.

When we enrolled Mark and Sandy in public school, we also enrolled them in the local Talmud Torah at the nearby synagogue, where they attended classes twice a week.

We also introduced the children to classical music by going to concerts and giving them music lessons – Mark played the violin and Sandy played the piano. She also took ballet lessons. I volunteered as a librarian at the school, and we lived a wonderful suburban life.

Once everyone had settled into a routine, I thought there might come a time when the children would ask me if I had finished high school. I never forgot how I had lied to get my job at M. Lowenstein and I didn't want to lie to my children. I found out that there were exams I could take at Temple University in Philadelphia that would grant me a high school equivalency diploma if I passed. I took the exam and was asked to come back for the results two weeks later. When I did, to my great delight and surprise, a gentleman handed me a State of Pennsylvania high school diploma and congratulated me on my success.

In 1964, Jackie was transferred back to New York, so we put the house in Broomall up for sale and went house-hunting on Long Island. He was going to be working in Douglastown, near the county line, and I began investigating school systems that were in reasonable commuting distance. We decided on Westbury in Nassau County, because their schools had the best reputation, but the cost of a one-family house in the area was astronomical. I told Jack, as he was now called, that I was willing to go back to work so that we wouldn't have to compromise on the quality of our children's education.

We found a house and enrolled the children in public school and Talmud Torah. We hired music teachers for the children and Sandy continued her ballet lessons at a school nearby. I earned extra money by working as a dressmaker, taking in alterations for the neighborhood ladies and soon built up a respectable clientele. I also did translations for businesses, under contract.

Every morning, I would get the family ready for their day, and once they were out the door, I would clean the house and then get to work until the children came home, when I would once again be a full-time mom. If I had to do something on deadline, I would go back to work only after they had gone to bed.

Two years later, we were transferred yet again, this time to an area in Maryland not far from Baltimore and Washington, D.C. We haven't moved since. All the while, Jack and I pushed our children to get the most of out their education, constantly reminding them how fortunate they were to have been born free in America, the country I cherish.

The United States, I told them, was a place where all children can dream and fulfill their dreams, no matter what their race or religion, without the fear of persecution. One day when I finished with my "lecture," fourteen-year-old Mark issued a challenge to me: "If education is so important, why don't you go back to school, Mommy?"

"Because I have to work with Daddy," I responded.

"No excuses, Mommy, if you are going to preach, you should preach by example."

"Do not be fresh," I retorted, but my son's words had an impact on me.

The next day, I went to the local college to find out if there was a way I could continue my education. When I found out I could, I began taking classes on a part-time basis. Several years later, at the ripe "old" age of forty-five, I earned my Bachelor of Arts degree, *magna cum laude*, from the University of Maryland. I pursued my graduate studies in education and was offered a position as a teaching assistant at the university. Two years later, I proudly received my master's degree and was asked to teach in the Montgomery County public school system. I accepted, and had a gratifying career teaching and helping young teenagers grow intellectually and as human beings.

Although I lived with my sad memories of the Holocaust, and had a mother who daily mourned her murdered family, I never shared these experiences with anyone at work or elsewhere. Throughout the years I concentrated on just being a good American, a good wife and mother, and a good member of the community. Then, one day in 1981 at the school where I taught, I came across a brochure promoting a book claiming that the Holocaust never happened, that the history of the Holocaust was a hoax. For me this was the moment of reckoning, the moment of recognizing that it was up to me and others who had lived under the frightening banner of the Swastika to speak up. I could no longer just live my life. I had a responsibility to give my testimony.

I joined a local organization of Holocaust survivors, Club Shalom, now called the Jewish Holocaust Survivors and Friends of Greater Washington. I became an active member and served for many years as co-president with my good friend, Nesse Godin.

While working as a high school language teacher, I collaborated with two fellow teachers, Bob Hines and Sue Shotel, in creating an in-service course for county teachers on the history of the Holocaust. In preparing the course the three of us thoroughly studied the historical precedents that led to the twentieth century's Holocaust. The course was approved by the State of Maryland. We started to teach it in 1983 and it is still beging taught today.

In the late eighties plans were drawn up for the building of the United States Holocaust Memorial Museum in Washington, D.C., to commemorate the victims and teach the history of the Holocaust to the public and professionals. I became involved together with other members of our Survivors' group as a speaker, telling my story as one who had been slated for annihilation, but managed to survive. I spoke at fundraisers for the project, bearing witness to the horrors of the Holocaust. I continued to remain actively involved with the United States Holocaust Memorial Museum in several areas after it opened. I volunteered as a development adviser and translator of Yiddish and French into English. I also worked with the Speakers' Bureau, traveling the width and breadth of the United States to various groups, but especially to young people at schools. Many groups visit the Museum, so there is often a need for a survivor on the premises to tell a personal side of the history. The ultimate goal of what the other survivors and I have done is to help people understand the cost in terms of human life and suffering that irrational hatred can cause.

When we were newlyweds, my husband found it difficult to understand the things that haunted me. And when the subject of the Holocaust came up, others found it difficult to understand as well. When the memories of those we lost surfaced and caused me pain, he tried to alleviate my pain by suggesting that I make an effort to forget. "Close the door and don't look back. This is a new life. Forget the past."

My husband's family had suffered some losses of distant family members, but since he'd never met them, and those closest to him were safe in the United States, the pain did not cut as sharply.

As time passed, my husband's understanding of my childhood experiences, my losses, and my family's losses deepened. He became very supportive of the work I was doing to bear witness. Jack became an active member as a friend of the Jewish Holocaust Survivors and Friends of Greater Washington, and a volunteer at the United States Holocaust Memorial Museum. Thus, we volunteered together, hoping that our work would make a difference by teaching people to live together in harmony and learn to stop the hate.

Through the years, no matter how busy I was, my thoughts would unwillingly return to those arrested and deported from Belgium by the Nazis. Mama continued to search and make inquiries to see if any of them might have survived the camps and perhaps returned to Brussels. She also tried to find out the fate of her family and Papa's family in Romania. I was preoccupied with thoughts of Heleneke and her beautiful blue outfit, who disappeared with her parents and brother. What happened to Uncle Alex, Aunt Lea and little Nounou? Did they survive and ever return to Belgium?

Nounou's face floats before my eyes every so often, even today. I loved that child, and miss him so very much. Whenever I am alone, when I walk through the museum, or stroll through a park, the faces of the lost are caught in my mind's eye, and I wonder and mourn. I know now that they were among the six million Jewish victims murdered by the Nazis. Perhaps, with museums and schools teaching the truth, perhaps humanity will understand and learn.

I never forgot Harreke and I never stopped searching for him. When the American Red Cross created a tracing service for Holocaust victims, I immediately contacted them and explained our relationship to Harreke. I gave them all the details – the name of the convent, the JDC home, and everything else I could remember, including the story of his family's disappearance. They finally found him. On January 1, 1998, the phone rang. A full fifty years since I had left him behind, Harreke, now a husband and father of two boys, and we were reunited at Los Angeles Airport.

Charlotte and Betty married and are proud parents and grandparents. Charlotte recently began sharing her memories with school children and volunteers at Nassau County's Holocaust Education Center. Betty, the youngest, does not speak about her experiences, because when Papa left Belgium in 1938, she was just two years old and can barely remember the details of our ordeal.

Eventually, I came to love my father and enjoyed being with him. He was a wonderful grandfather to our children. A heavy smoker, he developed emphysema, which took its toll on his lungs and his heart. Mama nursed him for several years, performing those duties with loving care. It distressed me, but I remained silent. I felt that it was unfair, that after the war years, after caring for the three of us, now, as she and Papa were supposed to be enjoying their lives together, with him caring for her, she became his nurse. Papa died at seventy-one in February 1980.

After Papa's death, it took a while, but Mama regained her optimistic spirit. Though she continued to mourn those she had lost, Mama enjoyed watching new generations of family grow in freedom, and greeted every new birth with hope. Mama died at eighty-five in April 1992. Her death saddened me greatly, but when I visit my parents' graves, I am at peace. No one killed them. They did not vanish without a trace like the millions of victims in the Holocaust. I know where they are buried and they rest in peace.

EPILOGUE

On January 20, 2006, Jack went out to collect the mail and came back to the house waving a large white envelope. He handed it to me and said, "This looks like an interesting letter from Belgium. I wonder what it is."

I opened the envelope and froze. Inside were copies of several documents that belonged to my beloved Uncle Alex and Aunt Lea Ciechanow, including copies of their identification cards with the infamous red stamp *Juif/ Jood* (Jew). I turned to stone, so shocked I couldn't feel a thing. Suddenly I could feel my heart beating again and I broke down and cried.

The Jewish Museum of Deportation and Resistance in Mechelen, Belgium, found the documents in its archives and located me as the next of kin. The museum is part of the former infamous deportation camp, where everyone was sent before going to Auschwitz. In the letter, the museum offered me the originals, "if I wished to have them."

I contacted them immediately by telephone to say, "Of course I want them." I wanted to hold in my hands the last items my dear Uncle Alex and Aunt Lea held in their hands before they disappeared into the depths with Nathan, my little Nounou.

I cannot bring back those I have lost; I cannot bring back the Six Million. All I can do is what I have done, and I am grateful that I was given the gift of a good family; the gift of an easy path compared to those others had to take during the war.

It is my hope that our witness to the truth of the Holocaust will stand to remind humanity that we must always remain humane and caring, and that we must stop the hate, for the sake of future generations.

IMAGES OF MEMORY

Zayde Moishe Genut, Romania,
perished in Auschwitz

Wedding of David Mendelovits and
Fani Davidovits-Genut (now deceased),
Belgium, 1929

Flora and Family,
Belgium, c. 1936

Flora, lower left, with relatives and friends,
Antwerp Public Garden, 1938.
All of these relatives and friends perished in Auschwitz

Fani with her three
daughters:
(left to right) Betty,
Flora and Charlotte,
Antwerp, 1937